to Join

A LONG RIDE HOME

A Billy Christian Adventure

RIDE!!

Michael Staires

ISBN: 1503389723
ISBN 13: 9781503389724
Library of Congress Control Number: 2014922487
CreateSpace Independent Publishing Platform
North Charleston, South Carolina

Acknowledgements

I'd like to thank the many people over the years who have encouraged me to put into writing the story that was told in the cabins and the A-frame and around the campfires at Shepherd's Fold Ranch. Thank you to my mom and dad, Don and Shirley Staires, who founded the camp and made it a place to begin the journey, explore the unknown, and discover destinies. Thank you to the many friends who helped me navigate the often-muddled publication process. To all those who have literally prayed this book into existence, you have my eternal gratitude. This book has been a journey of discovery for me every bit as much as for Son and Billy.

Dedication

I dedicate this book to my best friend, my wife Lainey. I'm thankful my long ride home has been with you at my side.

Preface

The desert darkness was complete. Other than the pinpricks coming from a billion stars, the only light was the small campfire sheltered against the wind at the edge of a grove of scrub pines and cedars.

The light from the fire lit the cowboy's weathered face. He wasn't that old but the strain of the last two and a half years shone on his face. He was tired. He was lonely. He'd done some great work. He'd been surrounded by good people on his journey. But he missed his family. He missed home. As great as good people can be they aren't family. The cowboy needed that closeness. He needed to be known, to be around those who *got* him. It was time to head back.

His horse, tied to a picket line between two old cedars, lowed deeply.

"What's that?" the cowboy said, almost to himself. "Yeah, I'll bet you're ready too."

The horse was a magnificent animal given to him by his father when his work first began. The horse was headstrong and the relationship was rocky at first with several fits and starts. But now the two moved and often thought as one. The horse seemed to know and anticipate what the cowboy wanted to do. And the cowboy couldn't imagine going a day without his horse, the closest thing he had to family out on this vast desert plain.

He took a deep breath and stoked the campfire with a crooked stick. Sparks rose up into the night sky as warmth from the hot red coals washed over him. He turned his collar up against the chill of the desert night. Just one more day on the trail and then…Home.

He knew the way by heart. Heck, his horse knew the way. He could drop the reins, tie himself in the saddle and go to sleep and the horse would find the way home. But the cowboy couldn't resist another look.

He reached inside his coat to the left breast pocket of his white shirt and pulled out a small book.

The book fit easily in the palm of his hand. Its edges were frayed and its pages yellowed—the ink on them faded. This book, this treasure, was the record of the work he'd done over the last two and a half years. Names, places, stories, rough drawings were all contained on the pages of this small journal. He put his finger on the scarlet thread that held his place and the book practically fell open to a certain page near the front. The cowboy angled it toward the campfire where he could get the most light and began to read. He smiled.

A couple of years ago he'd taken the time to write about Home. Not only did he describe the buildings and the people, he wrote about the land and the landmarks he'd need to look for on his way. He'd drawn a crude map detailing the lay of the land and the way back home. Looking over these pages now caused a big smile to cross his face, not that you could see it…hidden by his giant mustaches.

He closed the book tightly on the scarlet ribbon and placed it back in his pocket. He threw the last cedar branch from the pile on the small fire and scooted down to lay his head on his saddle. He covered himself with his duster and put his wide brimmed hat over his face. Tomorrow the trail would lead him back to his home and family.

"Sleep well Spirit," the cowboy said to his horse. "Tomorrow we'll be home."

CHAPTER ONE

The three buried their faces in the foul food. Old bits of corn, wilted lettuce and spoiled fruit stuck to their whiskers in their haste to get as much of the ugly slop into their mouths as possible. They pushed and shoved, each trying to get the best bits first. Manners were never a consideration. It was every man for himself…or rather every hog for himself.

The three little pigs who, because of this rich food every day had become the three huge hogs, lived on a farm nestled into a crook of the river in a beautiful valley surrounded by lush hills. On the farm lived a small family by the name of "Christian." This family was so small in fact that there were only two, an old man and a young boy. It was the boy's chore each evening to feed these noisy hogs.

The boy was Billy, and of all the things he had to do on the farm, he hated this chore most of all.

1

The hogs were big and smelly and mean. They spent all afternoon lying in the mud on the east side of the barn in the cool shade just waiting for their suppertime. They were bullies and although Billy would say he hated the hogs, the truth was he was scared of them. More than once they knocked him over in their headlong rush to get to their evening meal.

After each meal Billy and his Grandpa would scrape their plates into a bucket. By the end of a day or two the bucket was practically full of old oatmeal, crusts of dry toast, chicken bones, leftover orange juice, coffee grounds, droopy lettuce, old and dry shriveled fruit. It was Billy's chore to take the bucket full of the nasty stew out to the barn and feed the hungry hogs.

The barn sat behind the farmhouse and Billy would go out the back door of the house with the heavy pail bouncing against his leg almost always slopping its soupy contents on his pants. He would carefully climb the fence to the pigpen. The three hogs would all be on the other side of the barn dozing in the mud so Billy had to be very quiet to keep from waking them up and trampling him. He would dump the slop into the trough as silently as he could and then mix in some other pig feed. The sound of the food hitting the trough would awaken the hogs and they would come running around the corner of the barn. When Billy heard them coming he knew he only had seconds to toss the pail to the side and scramble up the fence to escape the stampede. Sometimes he made it; sometimes he didn't.

But even this horrible chore couldn't spoil Billy's favorite time of day. He would sit on the top rail of the fence overlooking the hogs. Over the sound of the chomping and snorting of the hogs he would watch the river flow into the distance as the sun slowly set. He dreamed of his future. It was always better than thoughts of the past, which held pain, confusion and rejection for Billy.

When Billy was still a baby, his parents decided they didn't want him anymore and decided to give him up to his grandpa to raise. His parents simply didn't care enough about him to want to raise him. Billy knew only too well that the opposite of love isn't hate. He had learned firsthand that the opposite of love is indifference. He'd long ago resigned himself to the fact that he may never know the reason why they'd given him up.

Billy's memories of his parents were only shadows that haunted the edges of his dreams. Now he lived with his grandpa way out in the country on this farm. They raised a few crops and kept some animals, including these horrible hogs.

Billy's escape from his own dark thoughts came each day as he sat on the top rail of the fence and dreamed of becoming a cowboy. That's what he really wanted to be. Sure he was thankful for Grandpa and thankful for the farm, but being a farmer was not what he wanted to do with the rest of his life. He wanted to ride the range and have the freedom to move when the mood struck him. A farm would always tie a man to the land, but Billy was more interested in what he might find on the other side of those hills in the distance rather than what was happening here at the farm.

The restlessness he felt was like an itch deep inside. He wanted to move, to travel, to see new things and meet new people. Being trapped on the farm and feeding the hogs was hardly the way he was going to scratch that itch.

There were times when he'd get up on the old mare, Blue, and pretend she was a beautiful horse with a shiny coat and a long, flowing mane. He'd dream he was out on the trail, driving cattle to a new destination. He would dream about life out on his own. He could imagine seeing the sunset each night in a new place and waking up each morning with a whole new day of discovery in front of him.

He would only ride as far as the river, but he'd pretend that he was miles, even days away. He would picture himself sitting tall in the saddle but in reality, he barely needed a saddle. Because of Blue's swayed back, all he had to do was nestle down between her withers and her tail bone and there was no way he was coming off.

Billy's idea of becoming a cowboy came from stories his grandpa told him of his dad's brother, Son. Billy had never met his uncle but Grandpa told him how Son traveled from place to place encountering new things and new people. In Billy's mind, Son had become the father he'd always wanted. Sure he'd never met his uncle but through Grandpa's stories, Son had come alive. Billy imagined that Son would love him and care for him—all the attributes Billy's father was never there to provide.

Often Grandpa would pause what he was doing, turn to Billy and say, "Someday Son will come riding right up that road. You'll see."

Grandpa loved to tell Billy all about Son and the mission he was on, helping others. He told Billy, "Son is a cowboy, but he doesn't take care of cows, he cares for people." Billy could hear in Grandpa's voice how proud of Son he was. Billy dreamed of living the same kind of life.

But Billy was discouraged because his dream of becoming a cowboy was just that, a foggy, distant dream. In reality he was just a farm boy sitting on a fence in charge of feeding a bunch of lousy hogs. A loud snort echoing out of the depths of the trough woke him out of his daydream. He looked up toward the sunset and saw a cloud of dust in the distance, the movement catching his eye.

Billy shielded his eyes from the setting sun so he could watch the growing haze of dust. The cloud got bigger and bigger as it got closer and Billy could now tell that it wasn't just the wind blowing up a dust devil or a stagecoach or a teamster's wagon. The dust cloud was coming from a single rider on a horse. And what a horse it was!

This horse was the most beautiful thing Billy had ever seen and while it was still too far away to see any real detail he could tell this horse was something special. It was dark as night and running so hard that its mane was flowing and its tail was blowing out behind, straight as a stick. The horse and its rider moved as one. Gradually the full gallop was reduced to an easy lope and, as the pair crossed over the bridge, they eventually slowed to a trot. Just when they reached the end of the farm's long driveway they hesitated for a moment before turning and coming up the drive toward Billy.

As they got closer, Billy could see the horse's coat was jet-black and glistening with sweat. The horse's nostrils were flared wide, sucking in great gulps of oxygen after the long run. It had a white blaze on its face and three white stockings. Both its mane and tail were long and wild. Its eyes were black and fierce. Once the rider reined to a halt, the mighty horse continued to prance in place, ready to take up the charge once again. The saddle was dark brown leather with silver accents and sat on a thick blanket woven with odd designs. There was a bedroll tied behind and a bulging saddlebag on each side. A rifle was tucked up in under one stirrup. Up in the saddle, riding this magnificent horse was a real live cowboy.

The first thing Billy noticed was the man's hat. It was probably white at one time but now was faded to a dusty off-white and had a thin braided leather hatband wrapped around the sweat stained crown. A single eagle feather was tucked under the band and lay flat on the wide brim. Years of exposure to harsh weather had stained the hat making it unique and one of a kind.

The man in the saddle was wearing a long gray duster reaching from his neck to his boots and spurs. The coat covered his clothes and kept them clean from the dust of the trail. Billy could just make out the white shirt under the black velvet coat collar. He had a faded silk scarf tied loosely around his neck. The man and horse slowly edged toward Billy. Big bushy mustaches hid the man's mouth.

Because of the wide brim of the hat, Billy couldn't see the cowboy's eyes until he stopped the horse and reached up with a gloved hand to tip his hat back on his head. His eyes were an intense, steely blue.

"Howdy," offered the stranger.

Billy's mouth was suddenly chalky dry. He struggled to swallow. "Uh, hi," stuttered Billy from his perch on the top rail.

"I'm looking for the Christian farm," said the cowboy with a great deep voice.

"Th…this is the Christian farm," stammered Billy.

The cowboy's face broke into a wide grin under the giant mustaches. "You must be Billy. Hey there boy, I'm your Uncle Son!"

CHAPTER TWO

Billy cried out, "Uncle Son!" and without another glance, he jumped off the fence and ran inside to tell Grandpa the news.

He ran up the path to the house and jerked open the old screen door that whapped loudly against the frame after Billy ran through. "Grandpa! Grandpa! Uncle Son is here!"

Billy knew where his grandpa would be and what he'd be doing. His routine rarely changed. Each evening after the dinner dishes were cleaned and while Billy was out with the hogs, Grandpa would take "The Book" down from the top shelf of the bookcase. It was thick and old and told the full history of the family. There were stories about the people who came way before Billy or his parents or Son or even Grandpa. It held the stories about Son and his travels. The back of this book was still full of empty pages. Grandpa told Billy that he would fill these pages with stories of his own someday.

Billy ran through the kitchen into the living room and saw Grandpa snoring in his huge rocking chair. His glasses were down on his nose and the old book was open on his lap but went flying as he jumped up, startled by the racket.

"What's going on?" Grandpa groaned...a good nap interrupted.

"Uncle Son is here!" blurted Billy. "He's outside by the barn on his horse!"

Grandpa smiled knowingly as he picked his glasses and book up off the floor. He got out of his chair and gently placed the book back on the shelf. "Well, go out and help him with his things. Let's get him in here and get him settled. I'll bet he's ready to get off that horse and have something to eat!"

Billy ran back out the back screen door, which sprung closed behind him with another WHAP! Whap, whap. He approached his uncle hesitantly, more than a little skittish around the powerful black horse. Billy looked up to see Son smiling through his thick mustaches. Son stood up in the stirrups and slowly climbed down from the horse and handed the reins to Billy.

"Want to help me get this horse unsaddled and brushed down for the evening?"

"Can I? This horse is awesome! What's his name?"

"This is Spirit. And you're right. He is a great horse."

Without thinking and with a boldness Billy didn't really feel, he asked, "Can I ride him?"

"Do you know how to ride?"

"Well, I ride Blue all the time," Billy said as he motioned with his chin toward the barn. "But Blue's not like Spirit; she's...uh...older."

"Tell you what, Billy. Someday soon we'll go riding together and I'll show you how to ride a horse like Spirit. You're right. He's different from Blue and you'll have some things to learn before you climb up on this one." Son said as he patted Spirit on the shoulder.

"I'd love that! Can we go for a ride right now?"

Son laughed. "Slow down a bit! Let's get him brushed down and get inside to see your Grandpa. We'll get started soon enough."

They led Spirit into the barn through the big double doors and all the way to the back where there was a small stall next to Blue. She turned and nodded at them in a quiet "hello," her ears pitched forward at the sight of the new horse in the barn.

The two slipped off Spirit's bridle and hung it on the peg on the back barn wall. Spirit plunged his nose into the trough of water in the corner and drank deeply. Next came the bedroll, saddlebags and rifle. Billy was in awe, tugging and pulling trying to get everything off the saddle.

"Slow down," chuckled Son. "We've got plenty of time. And be careful with those saddlebags. I just might have something in one of those bags for you and your Grandpa."

Billy's eyes grew wide as he carefully set the sad-dlebags on the ground in the corner of the stall. He reached for the rifle. It was heavy and awkward in his hands. He'd never held a gun before and was almost overwhelmed by the thought of it.

"Wow," Billy whispered. Then turning to Son, "Have you ever shot anyone?"

"I've only used the rifle when it was absolutely necessary. Anyone can pick up a rifle and pull the trigger. But it takes a wise man to know when and why to use it."

"Will you teach me how?"

"Sure I will. I'll teach you to ride and shoot and all sorts of things while I'm here."

They hung the huge saddle and blanket up on the rack to air out and turned their attention to the horse. Spirit was covered in sweat from the long dusty ride. Gently, Son showed Billy how to brush the horse's coat in long firm strokes. Gradually, the horse's luster began to return. They combed out the tangles in his long mane and tail. Spirit seemed to ignore them as he buried his nose in the hay trough

and began to eat. As they finished up, the horse murmured a quiet "thank you" for the brushing and the
two went into the house to see Grandpa.

That night passed in a blur for Billy. Grandpa
made up some leftovers for Son and the three of
them settled in the living room in front of the woodstove to catch up. Son picked up the saddlebags and
put them on his lap. He reached in for the gifts he'd
brought for Grandpa and Billy.

First, Son handed Grandpa the strangest looking
contraption Billy had ever seen. On one end was an
adjustable clamp and on the side was a wooden knob
mounted on a round crank.

"What is it Son?" Billy exclaimed.

"It's an apple peeler Billy. Let me show you how
it works. Go get me an apple!"

Billy ran in to the kitchen table where Grandpa
kept a big bowl of fruit. He grabbed a bright red apple
and returned to the living room where he handed it
over to Son who had clamped the peeler onto the
coffee table. After mounting the apple on the peeler
Son began to slowly turn the handle, which turned

the apple and engaged a small blade at the apple peel. Ribbons of red peel began to curl away and hang down from the fresh apple. The peeler also sliced the apple in a spiral as Son continued to turn the handle.

"Wow! Grandpa, that'll make baking apple pie a whole lot easier!" said Billy remembering the chore of peeling a big bowl of apples for pie.

"It sure will," said Grandpa. "Thank you Son. That's sure thoughtful of you."

Son smiled and winked at Grandpa.

"Do you have anything for me?" begged Billy.

"Well, let's see what we have in here," said Son as he reached into the bag and pretended to hunt around for something lost in the bottom. After making Billy wait a few moments, Son finally pulled something out from the depths of the saddlebag.

Billy's eyes grew wide. "What is it Son?"

Son held it up and turned it over in his hand. It appeared to be a piece of deer antler stuck down in a beaded leather sheath. But when Son pulled on the antler, a shiny blade emerged. It was a beautiful antler-handled hunting knife!

"Wow. Son! I love it! It even has a loop on it so I can wear it on my belt!" Billy jumped up and loosened his belt to strap the knife and sheath to his waist.

"Be careful Billy. It's sharp!" Son warned.

"Okay Son! Wow, thank you!"

"You're welcome Billy. I hope you enjoy it. It's been in our family for a very long time. Your grandpa gave it to me and now you have it to give to your boy."

"Thank you so much Son!"

"Son's right, Billy," said Grandpa. "And my dad gave that knife to me when I was a boy. You've got a family treasure there."

As the evening wore on, Billy settled down and laid on the floor as Son told stories of far away places with strange and interesting people. After what seemed like hours, he nodded off, unable to keep his eyes open any longer.

Through a sleepy fog, he could hear the men's conversation.

"The work is much harder now Dad," Son said sadly. "There are people out there who need our help like never before. Hurting people. Struggling people. There's way too much for me to do alone. I know this is my Destiny; it's what I was born to do. You've instilled that in me since I was Billy's age. But that doesn't make it any easier."

"That's true Son," said Grandpa. "Destiny is hard. Doing the right thing is rarely easy. But try living outside your Destiny, that's much tougher. Son, look at me, never forget, you were born for this moment in time."

Billy stirred and the two men both looked down at him dozing on the floor. Then they looked back up at each other. Volumes were exchanged between the two in their silent look. There's a kind of link between a Father and his son and they both recognized the power of being together. As Son looked down at Billy, he was surprised by the strong tug of emotion that caught him in his gut. He could feel the beginnings of an idea tickling the edges of his mind, then becoming clearer, stronger. He knew now why he was drawn back home. He knew why he'd ridden all those miles to make it back to the farm. He smiled to himself as he remembered that there's nothing quite like the thrill of a whole new mission in life.

Son shook out of his reverie when he realized his Father had begun to speak again. He turned his attention back to Grandpa.

"There's no denying and no escaping. We were put on this planet to accomplish big things Son and this is your big thing. Our enemy has stepped up his efforts lately. His attacks are becoming more and more ruthless."

"I know that for a fact," said Son. "Let me show you what I've encountered."

As the two men continued to talk their voices faded into the distance and like a heavy wave of warm water, Billy was washed away into a deep sleep. The last thing he remembered before falling asleep for good was seeing Son reach up and pull something from his shirt pocket. Was it a box or a book?

CHAPTER THREE

Billy woke up early to the sounds of voices downstairs. How did he get into his bed? He was so tired he didn't even remember walking upstairs to his bedroom. He played back his memory of the previous day, feeding the hogs, seeing the dust cloud, meeting Son, brushing Spirit, and falling asleep listening to all the stories. He rolled over and smiled as he saw the antler-handled knife that Son had given him on the small bedside table. It seemed so unreal.

He got up, quickly dressed and pounded down the stairs not wanting to miss a moment with Son. He found the two men in the kitchen, Grandpa frying up some bacon and Son with a coffee mug in his hand. The two turned as Billy came in.

"What are you two talking about?" Billy asked.

"We've got a lot to do before winter arrives Billy," Grandpa said. "We were just talking about the list of chores and the supplies we'll have to get from town. It's a good thing Son's here to help!"

Son took a sip of coffee and smiled. "I'm glad to be home. Just let me know what I need to do to help."

"Grandpa, can I take Son to town in the wagon to get the supplies?" Billy asked. "I'm sure he would love the chance to see how town has changed."

"I suppose so. Son, does that work for you?"

"Sure does," Son replied. "Let's get breakfast and then we'll head out."

Billy couldn't wait to spend the day with Son. After breakfast they scraped and washed their plates. Grandpa finished cleaning up while Billy and Son went out to the barn to get the wagon ready for the run to town. Together, they took the harnesses off the rack and put them on Blue. Billy showed Son how he laid out the reins and buckles so everything went on easily. He'd done this enough times he could do it with his eyes closed and he had fun showing Son how it was done. They led Blue out of the barn and hitched her to the wagon. Billy wanted to take Spirit but Son wanted to give him a rest after the long ride of the days before. They climbed up on the wagon and took their seats on the bench. Billy grabbed the reins, clicked his tongue and said, "Get up Blue!" Blue leaned forward into the effort. The trip to town had begun.

They crossed the small wooden bridge and turned right onto the road to town. Son turned to Billy and said, "I'll bet you love living on the farm don't you?"

"Well, I suppose so. I mean, it's okay I guess. I really like being out in the country and riding Blue and exploring the valley. But it can be really boring sometimes and I hate feeding those hogs!"

"You too? I didn't like that chore much either."

"Yeah!" agreed Billy. "First of all that slop is nasty. All that food mixed in the pail together? Yuck! And they stink! And besides that, those hogs are bullies! They knock me over just trying to get to the food first. I have to hurry to get up on the fence just to keep from getting trampled in the mud!"

Son laughed. He remembered feeling the exact same way when he was a kid. It seemed so long ago. Now the thought of feeding hogs didn't seem so bad. Sure, they might knock you down but not because they were mean. It was just because they were going for the food and didn't let anything get in their way.

Son turned to Billy, "Have you ever tried to think differently about those pigs Billy?"

"What do you mean? What good is it to change the way I think about something?"

Son smiled, remembering the lessons of his own youth. "The way you think about something is incredibly important Billy. Your thoughts are the roots for so much of everything else, like your attitudes, your habits, even your actions."

Billy looked down and appeared to take Son's words to heart. Son could almost hear the wheels turning in Billy's bright young mind, trying to make sense out of what he'd just heard.

"When you change the way you think, Billy, you can change the course of your life."

Billy squinted at Son and asked, "What do you mean Son? I don't get it. How can something as small as thoughts change my whole life?"

"Think carefully Billy. What's in your head before you act?"

"I suppose I'm thinking about what I'm about to do"

"Exactly Billy. No action just happens, unless it's instinct. Most all the time, we paint a picture of our actions in our mind before we take the first step. If we can change the painting, we can change the action. You follow?"

Billy looked down at Blue's hind-end, clip-clopping in front of him. "I guess so," he said, not entirely convinced.

"Just try it sometime. Try changing the way you think and just see if it changes the way you act."

Son knew that there would be many more difficult lessons to learn in the coming months for

Billy, but this first lesson was key. Mean hogs were one thing but mean people were quite another. On his mission, Son had experienced what "mean" really was. There was always someone speaking out against the work. Often, people would do more than just speak out; they'd go to almost any length to get him to stop his mission.

Son turned to Billy again. "So what's the next step Billy?"

"What do you mean, 'next step?'"

"When you grow up? Are you going to leave the farm?

"Yeah. I mean, I don't want to leave Grandpa but I don't want to stay here all my life either. What I really want to do is what you do! Traveling, seeing new places, meeting new people, every day different. That's what I want."

Son nodded. "It's not an easy life Billy. Not knowing what each day holds can be hard. The constant uncertainty can wear a guy out. The security and stability of home is a powerful thing and being so far away can sure be lonely."

"I know. I love Grandpa and I love this farm but I can't imagine being stuck here for the rest of my life. I want to get out of here and do something more than just be a farmer. It's okay for Grandpa but that's not what I want. I want to see stuff and do things. I listen to your stories and hear about all the places you go and I just want to bust! I'm tired of doing the same old things every day."

"I know," Son nodded. "I used to feel the same way. But I had to learn to be patient. Every day was an opportunity to learn the things I needed to learn so I'd be ready when the time came for me to start my own adventure."

"Will you teach me? I want to learn all I can!"

Son turned to look at his nephew. From the side it was easy to see the man Billy would become. Son saw his own brother in that profile. Adam, Billy's father, had chosen his own way. What a waste, he thought. Choosing self over others led to such an empty life.

It was in that moment, riding into town, that Son felt he'd passed another trail marker on this life's journey. He thought he was just coming back to the farm to rest and recuperate from months on the trail.

But the journey home was much more than that. Son was convinced that instead of helping all people, he was now to help Billy. He realized his new mission was to spend whatever time he had left to help Billy grow into the man he was supposed to be.

Billy felt Son's eyes on him. He pulled the wagon to a stop and turned on the bench to face him. Son took a deep breath and put his left hand on Billy's right shoulder. With a seriousness Billy hadn't seen before he said, "Billy, I'll do whatever I can to make sure you're ready to step into that dream."

Billy turned and looked his uncle full in the face. He couldn't understand the enormity of Son's words, but by the intensity of Son's look and the tone of his voice, Billy knew that something important had happened; a line had been crossed. With a lump in his throat he quietly said, "Thank you Son."

They both felt the significance of that moment. Billy turned his attention back to the road. He couldn't explain it but he felt older, more mature now. He sat up taller on the bench and pulled his shoulders back instead of hunching over. As Blue plodded down the road toward town, Billy tried to imagine what the future might hold.

Pulling into town was always exciting for Billy. The hustle and bustle, people hurrying back and forth, the sounds, the smells, all quite a change from the quiet pace of life on the farm. In town it seemed like anything could happen at any time. A celebration or a fight could break out at a moment's notice right in the middle of the road.

Son pulled the list of supplies out of his pocket and suggested they stop at the market first. Billy angled the wagon to the right side of the dirt street and slowly pulled up in front of a small shop with fruit displayed in the front windows.

They climbed down from the wagon and went up the few steps into the small store. It only took them a few minutes to get the things for the kitchen like flour and sugar, even some butter and cream. Their next stop was the hardware store for supplies like fence posts, barbed wire, nails, and some lumber. Billy took every chance to introduce his uncle to the folks in town.

In Billy's world, Son was famous and he enjoyed showing his celebrity uncle around town. But the more folks they saw, the more Billy picked up on something strange. The people acted suspicious and wary. Instead of being thrilled to see Son again, they were cool and guarded. Billy wondered what was going on. The two finished picking up the things on their list and after one more stop for some hard candy, they started back home.

As the calendar marched toward winter, the shorter days on the farm were filled from sun up until sundown accomplishing the long list of chores. Even a small farm like this required a lot of work. The three toiled each day fencing, repairing the stalls in the barn, fixing the old screen door, replacing the boards on the front porch, and burning the brush that had started to get out of control in the back pasture.

Son used every chore, every task as a teaching opportunity. Simple things like painting the barn or cleaning the harnesses and tack became valuable life lessons for his young nephew. The whole farm became their classroom. Every knotty pine board and every strand of wire became an object lesson.

Billy struggled from time to time and grew impatient with the work. When was he going to be able to ride a real horse and be a real cowboy? With Billy's long and loud sighs, it didn't take Son long to pick up on his discontent. He stopped and turned to his nephew, "What's wrong Billy?"

"I just don't like doing this stuff. When can we go on our ride? I'm tired of this boring little stuff. When are you going to teach me how to do the big things? I want to do the interesting things you do."

"Billy, things like painting and cleaning tack and yeah, even feeding the hogs may seem insignificant now but they're important because you're learning the lesson of doing the small things well. Come here a minute."

Son led Billy over to the workbench that ran along the inside wall of the barn. On the bench there were odd scraps of wood left over from some of the projects they were working on. Son picked up one of the odd shaped scraps and placed it on its edge on the bench in front of Billy.

"Now, let's pretend we're going to build a wall. Why don't you pick up another scrap of wood and put it on top of the one I put there." Billy found a piece and placed it on top of Son's piece but it toppled over immediately. Billy tried again but the blocks fell over again. The bottom piece was just too uneven to hold another piece of scrap on top of it. Billy shrugged his shoulders and took a deep breath in frustration.

Son smiled at Billy. "You see Billy, unless the bottom is even and level, everything you try to put on it will suffer. When you don't take care with the little things to make sure they're right, everything that follows can come crashing down. You've got to pay attention to the little things."

"In the same way, you don't just wake up one morning living the life you've always dreamed of. You build that life one day, one task at a time, just like building a wall with these blocks of wood. When you learn to do the little things well, you build a strong life you can be proud of, a life that will support and help others. When you're able work hard with the little things, you'll be ready to accomplish the bigger things. That's how good becomes great."

Billy thought about Son's lesson. "Is that why my thoughts are so important?"

Son smiled. "You're right Billy. When you're able to master your thoughts you're better able to master your actions. But there's more. Good actions, done over and over, lead to good habits. And a person with good habits can really begin to change things for the better."

Billy looked down at the task in his hand. He was struggling to scour rust off an axe. He looked up at Son then back to the axe. He set his jaw with determination and began to attack the rust with new vigor. He made up his mind; he was going to do the best job he could.

Son and Billy charged through the long list of chores. They sharpened the plow blade, noticing it would have to be replaced soon. They got the garden ready for the winter by turning over the soil and covering it with a deep pile of mulch and old dry manure. They cleaned the barn from top to bottom raking all the old moldy hay out of the loft and burning it. They put new hay up in the loft and stacked it neat and tidy. They even butchered the three hogs. To cure the pork and keep it from spoiling, they salted it first then stored it in the cellar for the long winter.

Although the work was hard, Billy was learning to love it. While they worked side by side, Son would tell about the places he'd been and the interesting people he'd met. He'd spent the last two and a half years traveling the countryside helping to build barns, fix a wagon wheel, plant crops, or stretch new fence. Sometimes he was simply there to hold someone's hand as they mourned a loss. Billy could see that Son's life wasn't just about riding and exploring new things and new places. Son's life was all about serving others.

After dinner, Son would stoke the wood stove and sit in his favorite chair. Billy would lay on the floor pretending to read a book, but he was really waiting for Son to say the words he longed to hear, "Let me tell you a story…" Grandpa would rouse himself from his evening catnap and Billy would sit up. Son would lean forward and with a twinkle in his eyes he'd say in his raspy voice, "I remember one time…" and he'd launch into another tale of his adventures.

Under the soft glow of the lantern, Son's eyes would dance as he wove his fascinating tales. And as Son leaned forward, Billy could just make out the outline of something in Son's shirt pocket. He wasn't positive, but it looked like a small book.

CHAPTER FOUR

Winter nights in the old farmhouse could be icy. Billy would wake each morning buried deep under the heavy quilts of his bed. He was able to see his breath in the chilled air of the attic bedroom. He'd lay wrapped in his warm cocoon as long as he could before throwing back the quilts. He'd jump out of bed, grab his pile of clothes and run downstairs to dress in front of the wood stove. Grandpa would bring him a mug of hot chocolate to drink while he waited on his breakfast.

One morning he came downstairs and found Grandpa in the quiet kitchen alone. He noticed that Son wasn't at the table drinking coffee like he usually was. Billy asked his grandpa, "Where's Son?"

"He's already up and out. He went to the barn early to saddle up Spirit. Said he had someplace to go."

Billy ran upstairs and put on his warmest socks and boots. He ran to the back door, got his coat and hat off the pegs and bolted out the door. A ribbon of light lined the distant eastern hills as the sun started its daily climb in the sky. The cold air froze the inside of Billy's nose as he breathed deeply. He quickly pulled on his gloves before his hands froze. Once the sun came up, the day would warm a bit, but for now the nighttime chill was still lingering in the air.

Billy slid open the big barn door just wide enough to slip through. Once inside the barn it took a moment for his eyes to adjust to the early morning darkness. He loved this old barn and could navigate his way around even with his eyes closed. He heard something and saw movement back in the corner in Spirit's stall. Sure enough, he could just make out the shape of Son going through the motions of saddling up Spirit. Son looked up and smiled at Billy. "You want to go for a ride with me?"

"Yes! But I only have Blue to ride."

"That's okay. Blue is a fine horse. And she's all the horse you need right now. She'll show you how to ride if you'll just let her."

"Oh, okay," Billy reluctantly agreed. He wanted a horse like Spirit not an old nag like Blue. He was doing his best to change the way he thought about things but it was hard. He trusted that Son knew best.

They gave both horses a couple of scoops of oats while they saddled them up. Then after going back inside to bundle up for the cold ride and grab some food for the trail, they took off. They crossed the river at a place in the shallows and headed up into the hills. They rode along narrow trails through the bare aspen groves, across trickling streams and over rolling hills. They rode further than Billy had ever ridden before. Blue was doing just fine but Billy's rump was starting to ache.

But they had more riding to do. All along the way, Son showed Billy how to lean forward when the horses went uphill and lean back when they were going downhill. He showed him how to stand up in the stirrups when his backside ached. He showed him how to hold the reins and steer the horse left and right. When they came to open land they would gallop the horses a little, just for a change of pace. Son showed Billy how to put his weight in the stirrups and move with the horse as if he were in a rocking chair. Billy began to have a whole new appreciation for Blue and for her strength and speed. He was learning to ride like a real cowboy! He realized that, in the past, when he thought about Blue as a nag, she was a nag. But now that he had changed his thoughts toward her, she seemed like she'd become altogether different horse. It occurred to Billy that Blue wasn't the one who had changed. He was the one doing the changing.

Billy was finally getting a taste of what he'd wanted to do since he was a little boy. This is the life he'd dreamed of, riding the trail and exploring new things. Around every bend was a new sight. The sky looked different. The trees looked different. Even the brown winter grass fascinated him. He was cold and sore but he was having the time of his life. He was on an adventure! He'd never been this far away from the farm.

Billy imagined himself looking just like Son. Instead of his knit cap and plaid wool coat, he saw himself with a sweat-stained, wide-brimmed hat and long duster coat just like Son. He stood up in the stirrups and even thought Blue was beginning to look more and more like Spirit.

The trail continued to climb through the trees and high up into the hills. Son and Spirit led the way with Billy and Blue plodding along behind. Occasionally they'd stop and Son would pull a small book out of his front pocket and look at the dog-eared pages like he was checking a map. This was the very same small book Billy had noticed from time to time peeking out of Son's pocket. But he'd never actually seen Son pull it out and look at it. The book was old with a cracked black leather cover and faded red spine. Billy could see a frayed scarlet ribbon peeking out from between the pages.

Son was checking something intently while sitting still as a statue on Spirit's back. He looked up from the yellowed pages and examined the trees in front of him.

Son turned in his saddle and pointed to what looked like a splash of red paint on the bark of a white birch tree alongside the trail. "This is what we're looking for Billy." As Billy rode by the tree and looked closer he noticed that it wasn't a haphazard splash of color, it was a handprint as if someone had dipped a hand in red paint and slapped the tree.

"We need to follow the path of the red hand."

The red handmarks led them higher into the hills. They would see the red hand on trees and big rocks along the trail. It was like a treasure hunt and Billy watched for the mark, giving him something to think about other than the cold.

By the time they reached a high ridgeline Billy was ready to get off his horse and stretch his legs. His feet were like blocks of ice. The red marks led them to a mountaintop clearing with a great view of the valley below. A river lay along the valley floor like a silver ribbon. Billy wondered to himself if this might be the very same river that ran through their farm. Along a bend in the river, at the edge of a grove of cedars, they could see a small group of Indian lodges. Fifteen to twenty teepees dotted the meadow between the trees and the water. From their vantage point high up on the ridge they could just make out people going about their day gathering firewood and fresh water.

Son reached back into his saddlebag and pulled out a short brass tube. After pulling on one end, the tube snapped out longer. He took a long look through one end into the village below. He passed it over to Billy, who'd never even heard of a telescope, much less looked through one. He held the glass up to one eye and closed the other. As he looked through the telescope, fuzzy distant objects began to come into focus and take shape.

Now he could easily see a couple of scrawny dogs fighting over some scraps and children playing a game with sticks and a ball. The smoke from the cook fires curled up from the top of their lodges into the cold windless sky.

Billy passed the telescope back to Son who pointed to the small village below and said, "That's where we're headed Billy. Those folks were forced from their homeland and have been made to live in this valley. They're not going to be able to move around like in the past. They're accustomed to following the animals they hunt, like buffalo, elk, beaver and deer through these mountains. Now they have to learn to be settlers and get used to staying in one place. They need someone to show them how, and that's our new mission."

CHAPTER FIVE

They made their way down the trail, across the river and into the clearing. The people stopped what they were doing and looked up at them with curiosity. The children ran up to get a closer look. Even the dogs stopped their tug-of-war and began to bark. The men came out of their lodges and Son got off Spirit and began to speak to them in their own language…a language Billy had never heard before. He was astonished. How did Son know how to speak to them? Billy noticed something else; even though Billy and Son were strangers to these people, they were warm and open without a hint of the suspicion that Billy noticed among the people in town.

A couple of the women took their horses for some much-deserved hay and water while the men motioned for Son to follow them into the main council lodge. Billy couldn't help but notice the red hand splashed to the right of the flap that led into the huge tepee. He started to follow but one of the elders put a hand on his shoulder to stop him from entering the council. The elder wasn't sure how old Billy was and young boys didn't sit at council. Billy looked up at Son who looked at the elder and said something to him. The elder removed his hand, nodded to Billy and the three entered the council together.

Once Billy's eyes adjusted to the dim light, he could see there was a warm fire burning in the center of the room and thick bearskins scattered around to sit on. Billy and Son were given bowls of hearty stew to eat and hot tea to drink. They were shown to a place on the floor where they could sit. With the combination of the fire, the warm furs and the hot food, Billy began to slowly thaw out.

Billy looked around the circle of men, the light from the fire brightening their faces. He'd seen Indians before but he'd never been this close. Seeing them here in the lodge he realized how different they were in person than in the silly stories that the other boys in town told. He understood now just how ignorant those boys had been, telling stories about things they knew nothing about. The Indians' skin was darker than his and they wore their hair longer.

Each of the elders in the circle wore feathers in his hair and necklaces of colorful beads and animal claws. Several of the men had symbols tattooed on their forearms and hands. Billy thought they were a strange and beautiful people.

Everyone sat cross-legged around the fire on the furs with their deerskin breeches and knee-high moccasins. They wore soft leather tunics with leather laces at the neck and many had thick furs wrapped around their shoulders to ward off the cold. These weren't "poor Indians," thought Billy. They were a proud people who had been forced to live a life they weren't used to living.

Billy looked through the smoke across the circle to a man with a beautiful blanket wrapped tightly around his shoulders. The man was, by Billy's estimation, the oldest man in the room. He was smoking his pipe and listening to the quiet conversation. He watched Son closely and waited for his guest to finish his stew. When Son finished eating he laid down his spoon. The old man raised his hand to quiet the elders. In a low voice he began to speak. From the first syllable of the strange language, Billy knew this man had to be the chief of the tribe. He carried himself with authority and strength; it was obvious this

45

man was in charge. The circle of men listened quietly and respectfully, barely making a move.

Billy had no idea what the chief was saying so Son
leaned over and began to translate in a quiet whisper.

"That man is Chief Red Buffalo. He's been the
chief elder of these people for a very long time. He's
telling the story of his people and how they've come to
be here in this valley. His heart breaks at being forced
to live in this place, not allowed to roam the land. His
people are used to following the buffalo and elk and
other game as they hunt throughout the year."

"You see Billy," Son continued. "Land ownership
is a foreign concept to these people. To them, God
gave the earth and all that is in it for all of us to share.
To imagine that one person or one group of people
would lay claim to a piece of property is something
they simply don't understand."

"Two years ago they were wintering on a piece of
land much like this one. They had shelter in the trees
and an abundance of fresh water. They were following the elk and buffalo and using the site as a kind of
home base, but the white settlers had their eyes on
the land; that meant roads and railroads and homes

and other settlers, and they didn't want to share the land with the Indians so they forced them to move away. Soldiers came and led them on a forced march to this valley. And even though it's pretty and peaceful here right now, there's trouble brewing."

Son glanced back over to Red Buffalo to listen, then murmured, "Hmm. that's not good." He continued the translation, "There have already been a couple of troubling visits from some of the townspeople. They have their eyes on this valley for the railroad route."

"Red Buffalo is willing to stay here and learn to settle for the peace of his people but he's very concerned about what the white man might do." Son turned his attention back to the chief.

Red Buffalo stopped talking and passed the pipe around the circle to Son who bowed his head and then drew from the pipe deeply and passed it back to the chief. Son cleared his throat and began to share with the council in their own language. Son told the elders who he was and who Billy was and that they were there to help. Son wanted them to know how much he cared for them and how sorry he was that they'd been forced off their land. He told them he'd help them anyway he could, but he emphasized that going to war with the townspeople was not the answer.

Chief Red Buffalo listened. When Son was finished speaking, the chief nodded, put the pipe to his lips and inhaled deeply. The elders around the council circle turned to one another and nodded. They had serious concerns about the future but they were going to accept Son and Billy and their offer to help. They stood and embraced all around. The elders gave gifts of necklaces and other jewelry to Son and Billy. Son walked across the circle to stand in front of Red Buffalo. He reached down and unbuckled his belt and slid it off from around his waist and offered it to Red Buffalo as a gift. The elders noticed and a hush fell over the council. Red Buffalo took the belt and embraced Son.

Red Buffalo then took off his own belt and gave it to Son but as he was handing it over, he removed a large hunting knife from a sheath attached to the belt. The blade was shiny and sharp and the handle was made from an elk antler. Billy inhaled sharply. This knife was very similar to the one Son gave him. The chief took the knife and lifted it up, saying something Billy didn't understand. Then he placed the blade of the knife in his right hand and drew it quickly, slicing his palm. Billy winced. As the chief's hand began to bleed, he passed the knife across to Son who did the same thing, cutting his right palm. The two clasped their right hands together and embraced.

The elders began to sing. It was a beautiful, somber, song and even though Billy couldn't understand a word, he knew that something very special had just happened. There was something about this chorus of men's voices that touched Billy's heart. The hair stood up at the back of his neck and his knees grew weak. He felt hot and faint but he took a deep breath and steadied himself. This was a very sacred and important rite for these people and the last thing Billy wanted to do was fall over. Without knowing the meaning of a single word, Billy understood that Son had just promised to help these people no matter what might happen.

As Son and Red Buffalo turned to face the council of elders, the old man withdrew a large folded cloth from inside his tunic. There was a hush around the circle as the chief held the cloth over his head. Billy could see that it was covered with strange symbols and images. The chief closed his eyes and sang a verse of the sacred song by himself. His voice was deep and low. When he finished singing, he tore the cloth and gave one half to Son. He took the other half and wrapped it around his bloody palm. Son took his half of the cloth and did the same.

The council broke up and Son made plans for a return trip. They made their way back outside the lodge and mounted up for the long ride home. The women had repacked their saddlebags with food and gave them a skin of cold water. They mounted up and headed up the mountain on the long trail back. The trip home seemed shorter. Billy could still hear the haunting melody of the council chorus in his head. His mind was swirling with questions for his uncle. He finally spoke up.

"Son, I want to help you but I don't see how I can. I don't know the language and I don't understand their ways."

"Billy, you can help more than you know. You've lived on the farm with your grandpa almost all your life. You know how a farm is supposed to operate. You know how to live life as a settler. And besides, I'll always be there to help you and we can start working on the language right away. You'll pick it up in no time at all."

Billy fell silent, his mind a blur. He held Blue's reins in one hand and took a bite of Indian bread with the other. He had so many questions.

It was cold and dark when they crossed over the river and made their way back to the farm. They rode into the barn and climbed down off the weary horses. Billy brushed Blue just like Son taught him and made sure she had plenty of good grain to eat before going inside to warm up and get ready for bed.

It had been an exciting but exhausting day. Billy had never spent that much time on a horse in one day in his life. As he got out of his clothes and put on his pajamas he thought about the people in the village. Would they be warm tonight? He got in bed and pulled the quilts up under his chin and felt their weight on his chest. He thought about those bearskins and he could smell the smoke from the council fire on his skin. As his eyelids grew heavy, he closed them and began to dream. In his dream he was riding a horse but it wasn't Blue, it was Spirit. He was riding Spirit on a winding trail through yellow aspens that were each marked with a red hand. He could hear the voices of the council singing their ceremonial song. He watched as the strange symbols embroidered on the cloth danced across his mind.

CHAPTER SIX

Over the next weeks, Billy and Son rode over the hills and valleys to the Indian village many times. Son no longer needed to consult the mysterious little book and they didn't need to look for the red hand any more. Even the horses had memorized the way.

With each trip Billy found he was beginning to understand the language a little more. He couldn't speak it yet but now he could understand the gist of what the Indians were saying. He looked forward to the long rides through the hills, spending time with Son and helping the people of the village. The process was slow but steady. They were building fences for the livestock and marking off sections around the village to plant crops once it was time. Billy found himself drawn to these people. It was like he had a big magnet down deep inside him that pulled him toward the Indians.

The more he got to know them the more he was able to identify with them. He felt like he understood them. He was no longer going along just to be with his uncle, now he was going because he truly wanted to help the people.

Something else began to happen. Instead of daydreaming of becoming a cowboy, Billy began to daydream about new ways to help the Indians. He would imagine things he could contribute to the effort. He felt his attitude beginning to shift as his confidence in his ability to accomplish this mission grew.

He thought about ways to improve what they were already doing in their work. With each trip over, Billy had new ideas and Son came to rely on Billy and his fresh insight. Billy changed the way they packed the supplies in the wagon so they could get more in each load. And it was Billy's idea to change the direction they were planning on planting the crops. He suggested that if they planted east to west instead of north to south that the crops would get more of the summer sun. Son swelled with pride at Billy's idea. His careful lessons were beginning to pay off. But more than that, Son realized that Billy was gaining confidence. Billy was much more inclined to give his opinion, to risk being wrong. It was then that Son knew that Billy was becoming much more than just an apprentice. He was becoming a partner.

With ideas like this, the Indians no longer looked at Billy as merely Son's nephew "along for the ride." Billy was becoming a source of knowledge just like his uncle. There was no doubt Billy was becoming much older and more mature than his young years would indicate.

Every couple of weeks they'd have to schedule a trip to town for a fresh load of supplies, some things for the farm and always a few things for their projects at the village. On these trips, Son and Billy would sit in the wagon and outline their plans for helping the Indians. Spring was on its way and that meant turning over the ground and planting crops. There was a lot of work ahead.

Winter began to slowly loosen its grip on the land. Spring was coming and each new day brought the promise of new adventures. But with each trip to town, Billy began to notice, even more, the icy stares of the townspeople. It was subtle at first but over time became more and more obvious.

On one trip to town Billy walked out of the drug store with a bag of candy. He was counting his change when a voice called out to him from the alleyway. He peered into the shadows.

"Hey, Billy."

Billy jumped. It was Eli, an older boy he'd seen around town.

"Whatcha doin'?"

Billy didn't know Eli well and was surprised he was even talking to him. "Hey Eli. Just pickin' up some supplies for the farm. What're you doin'?"

"Nothin'," Eli said as he looked up and down the street cautiously. He lowered his voice, "What're you guys doing out there with the Indians anyway?"

"What do you mean? We're just trying to help them out. They hardly have anything. We're just helping them get up on their feet."

"Are you crazy?" Eli almost yelled before remembering where he was and lowering his voice back to a whisper. "You better stop it before someone gets hurt!"

"What? We're not doing anything wrong! Who would get hurt?"

"Say brainless...don't you get it? There are folks here in town who don't want those Indians around. They want that land for themselves. I heard my dad saying that they want to build another settlement out there and need the valley for a railroad. They won't abide you and your uncle showing them a kindness."

"I don't see what the big deal is."

"Well, don't say I didn't warn you. And don't you dare tell anyone we talked!" And with that Eli slunk back into the shadows of the alleyway.

Billy made his way back to the wagon. He climbed up and settled on the bench next to Son, who was already there reading a book. He could tell Billy had something on his mind.

"What's with the long face?" Son asked. "You look like you're carrying the weight of the world."

"I just saw Eli. He was nervous as a cat. He told me why people here in town are acting so funny around us. He said folks have their eyes on that land…the land where the Indian village is. He said they don't like us helping them. I remember you telling me that on our first trip to the village but I guess I was hoping it wasn't really like that. It's not true is it Son?"

"Billy, when you try to help someone there will always be opposition. Darkness is always lurking— trying to overcome the light. That's just the nature of things."

"But how can we make them understand? We're only trying to help! We're not doing anything wrong."

"Some folks make up their minds about what is right and what is wrong and they won't budge. They don't want their lives interrupted. They like things just the way they are and they'll stand against any- thing that smells like change."

"What are we going to do Son?"

"We'll continue our work. We promised we'd help those folks and that's what we're going to do." He showed Billy the now faint scar on his right palm. "We promised…I promised. We'll just have to be careful and keep a close eye out."

Each retreated into their own thoughts as Son directed Blue down the street. The air between them buzzed with the new-found tension of what the coming days might bring.

After pulling the wagon up in front of the hardware store and tying Blue up to the hitching post, they climbed down and went inside with their long list of supplies. But from the moment they came in the door they could feel a change. Other shoppers quickly left and Mr. Gentry, the shopkeeper watched them closely with an evil eye.

Billy finally couldn't stand it anymore. He cleared his throat loudly and asked Mr. Gentry, "What's going on around here? You got a problem with us?"

Mr. Gentry narrowed his eyes at Billy and straightened his starched white apron. He pointed to the paper in Son's hand, "I'll wager half the stuff on that list ain't even for the farm is it? Neither one of you are welcome in here if you're going to buy supplies to help them Indians."

Billy started to snap back a response but Son put his hand on Billy's arm and replied, "I thought you were in business to make money Mr. Gentry. I thought you'd sell to anyone with enough money to pay. Folks should be free to do whatever they want with what they buy."

"Look Son," Mr. Gentry said, "I've known your family for a long, long time and for all those years y'all've been good customers. But you've gone too far with this business of helping those Indians. I know you been away for a while. You need to know that times have changed. Things are different now." Mr. Gentry threw his shoulders back defiantly and said, "Factually, I own this store and I can refuse service to anyone I want. I want you and the boy out of my store before I call the sheriff! I know what you aim to do with these supplies and I won't be a party to it!"

Billy couldn't believe his ears. He'd grown up in this town and thought he knew these people. He'd even helped Mr. Gentry sweep out his store from time to time.

Son turned and whispered, "Come on Billy. Let's go. This man has a busy store to keep. We'll have to figure another way to get the supplies we need." They turned and left the store.

"It's no use!" Mr. Gentry called out after them. "The whole town's united on this! No one's going to sell to you! You're blocked out!"

Folks out on the sidewalk stared at them as they untied Blue and got back up in the wagon. Son snapped the reins. With an eerie silence they rolled down the street toward the edge of town feeling the suspicious stares on their backs.

Sitting on the wagon bench beside Son, Billy balled his fist and hit his own knee. "I can't believe this! Mr. Gentry made me so mad! If you hadn't stopped me in there, I don't know what I might've done!"

"That would've been a shame Billy. Acting on impulse is rarely wise. The kind of thoughts you're having toward Mr. Gentry only lead to foolish actions and destructive habits. They surely don't lead to greatness. If you want to grow up to be the man you were created to be, you'll have to learn to rein in those wild thoughts."

Son went on, "Billy, a man with no self-control is like a town with no law. There's only chaos and destruction."

Billy knew his uncle was right. He murmured a quiet, "I know. I'm sorry I acted that way. I'll do better." Son gave a smile of understanding and snapped the reins on Blue's rump and they continued on their way through town.

Just past the funeral parlor and behind the livery stable at the edge of town was an old homestead. There was a broken down old house and some corrals and assorted out-buildings. This was Ned's place. Billy had never met Ned but had heard lots of stories about him. Everyone said Ned was crazy. He'd lived in that shack at the edge of town for as long as Billy could remember. He collected old things like used tools and equipment and broken down old wagons and tack. He had sheds full of glass bottles and pieces of wooden chairs and other furniture. There were rusty iron gates and bed frames and lanterns. It all looked like worthless junk to Billy.

A pack of barking dogs met them as they pulled up in front of Ned's place. The old man came out onto the porch stretching and scratching his backside. He looked like he'd just gotten up from a nap.

Ned looked crazy enough. He appeared to be 100 years old with his long wispy gray hair and matted beard. He wore a stained undershirt and torn pants tucked down inside his tall worn out old boots. He pulled his suspenders up over his shoulders and yelled, "QUIT YER YAPPIN'!" at his dogs. They gradually stopped their ruckus and hesitantly headed back under the porch to resume their afternoon nap.

Ned squinted and eyed them up and down. "What can I do for you two?" Ned said.

"Hello Ned," said Son. "How're you doing?"

"Not too bad. Chilly reception in town?" Ned said through a toothless grin. Billy was surprised. Ned didn't sound crazy at all. Sure he looked weird and acted a little crazy, but otherwise, Ned seemed completely normal. He was a lot nicer to them than anyone else in town had been.

Son turned and looked over his shoulder, then looked back at Ned and smiled. "Yeah, you might say that."

Ned picked a scrap of food out of his thick beard and put it in his mouth. Smacking his lips he said, "I figured it was bound to happen. They've been whining and groaning for weeks about you and Billy and the work you've been doing. People say things. They assume I'm crazy and can't understand. I've even heard them speculating there might be gold out there, which would make them want that land even more. They've been talking about blocking you out for a while now…I guess they've had enough of you two helping those poor folks."

Son reached up and pushed his hat back on his head. "Yeah, they don't understand. They're scared and upset. But we've got lots more to do out there and need some supplies. Can you help us?"

"Sure I can. I think it's a shame 'bout those folks gettin' forced out of their way of life. It just ain't right. But I never knew what I could do about it. Truth be told, I been a little scared myself to stand up to Mr. Gentry and the others. I'm glad yer doin' somethin' about it. I'll help you any way I can."

Son smiled and winked at Billy. They climbed down out of the wagon and followed Ned out behind one of the old sheds. Under a stack of tin panels there were coils of used barbed wire. Ned also had wooden boxes full of old fence staples along with stacks of used fence posts. They saw rusted plows and cracked and dry leather harnesses. It all needed some work but it was usable.

"You can pick through this stuff here and take whatever you need," Ned offered.

"Much obliged Ned. But I want to pay for it. I don't expect you to just give it to us for free," Son replied.

"Well, okay then," Ned replied. "Let's get what you need loaded in the wagon and we'll figure out a fair price. I'm just glad to help."

"I know Ned," Son said. "And we thank you very kindly."

There was more here than they thought at first. They found several more rolls of used barbed wire stacked against the shed and grabbed a couple of boxes of staples and all the posts they could load. While they were at it, they each took an armload of odds and ends they thought they could use and loaded them into the wagon.

Son and Ned agreed on a price and Son paid him, adding a little extra. Son and Billy got up in the wagon and headed to the farm on a back road around town so they wouldn't have to double-back and endure the dirty looks they'd get on a ride back through town. It was a quiet ride back. They both realized the shift in things. There was a new element of danger and their minds were spinning.

Back at the farm, they pulled the wagon up to the barn just as the sun was setting. Tomorrow they'd take the supplies to the Indians and help them build pens for their livestock. Billy and Son were exhausted and just left the things in the wagon, unhitched Blue, brushed her down, put some grain in the trough for her and went inside for some dinner.

Grandpa was waiting with a big pot of stew but after the trip to town, Billy didn't feel much like eating. The conversation with Eli and the confrontation with Mr. Gentry and the townspeople had been upsetting. Billy had never seen that kind of ugliness, especially in folks he thought were friends. He picked at his food but after a while he gave up and asked to be excused.

After dinner Billy fell asleep on the floor in front of the woodstove half listening to the soft murmurs of Son and Grandpa's conversation. It had been a long hard day. Billy had seen and heard things that troubled him and that he didn't understand. Why wouldn't the people in town want to help the Indians? Billy drifted in and out of sleep and finally staggered upstairs to bed. He pulled his covers up, rolled over and fell into a fitful sleep.

CHAPTER SEVEN

Spring was coming but winter was still holding on. Billy hated getting up early, especially on these cold mornings. He'd surprised himself by being awake before sun-up. Taking a deep breath, he pulled back the layer of warm quilts to put his bare feet on the chilly floorboards. He was still troubled about the trip to town. His dreams had been filled with hateful glances and disapproving faces. The dream led him to terrible thoughts about the folks in town. He knew the thoughts were wrong but he had a tough time reining them in. The longer he lay in bed, the harder it was to fight off the nagging, destructive thoughts. He might as well get up out of bed and start the day.

He dressed and on the way downstairs he had a flash of inspiration. He thought of the old Colt revolver Grandpa kept in his desk. He quickly detoured to the roll-top and grabbed the gun and holster from the bottom drawer. He belted it around his waist and cinched it tight. He knew it was against the rules to take the gun but it made him feel so grown up. Plus, you never knew what you might find when you're out on the trail, he thought. He looked down at himself and smiled. Now he felt like a real cowboy! He went to the back door, put on his coat and hat and slipped silently out of the house and hurried to the barn. He saddled up Blue and rode out just as the light of the new day was peeking over the ridge east of the farm. Just feeling the weight of the gun at his hip made him sit up a little taller in the saddle.

He rode down to the river then turned and headed upstream along a trail he hadn't been on since last year. A late-season dusting of snow had fallen overnight, just enough to cover the ground. As Blue plodded along the trail, Billy became lost in his thoughts.

The distant memory of his parents drifted through his mind. Growing up with Grandpa, he'd only known love and kindness. His parents' apathy toward him was troubling but it was the loathing he sensed from the townspeople that kept him awake at night. He tried to keep his thoughts positive like Son had taught him, but it was proving a tough task.

Suddenly, he was yanked back to reality when Blue stopped short and jerked her head up. Her ears were pointed forward; she was on high alert. She didn't move a muscle, staring straight ahead.

In the stream ahead was a giant momma grizzly bear. Normally a bear would be hibernating this time of year and Billy wondered what might have roused her from her winter's nap. Thankfully she was too caught up in her effort to catch a fish for breakfast to pay any attention to Billy and Blue.

"Whoa, Blue," whispered Billy. He patted her shoulder lightly, encouraging her not to make any sudden moves. A sound in the bushes behind him made him turn in the saddle. A small grizzly bear cub emerged from the thicket. No doubt the cub had grown bored watching his momma fish and decided to explore the riverbank. Now Billy found himself in the worst place possible, between a momma grizzly bear and her cub.

He knew he had to get out of there, but how could he back up without being noticed? He tugged on the reins to back Blue up just a bit so he could turn around on the narrow trail. Blue made a low rumble of protest deep down in her throat. The cub heard the noise and stopped his rummaging in the bushes. He squeaked a tiny cub growl, barely enough to hear over the rushing stream. But it was loud enough. The momma grizzly jerked her head out of the water. She saw Billy and Blue. She stood up to her full height and roared her loudest roar!

Billy pulled the reins hard to get Blue turned around. But Blue was badly spooked and Billy's pulling the reins only confused her. She reared up in her tracks causing Billy to lose his balance and fall back out of the saddle, landing on the ground with a thud. He turned his head just in time to see Blue gallop up the trail back toward the farm.

Billy turned around. The momma bear was still standing to his left midstream, roaring her warning. The cub was to his right and still bawling loudly. The louder the cub got, the madder the momma grizzly got. Billy scrambled to his feet and began to put one foot carefully behind the other keeping his eyes glued to the grizzly. But the cub was moving too and Billy still found himself between the momma and baby.

The cub suddenly cried out and Billy turned to see why. The whimpering cub was sitting on his haunches licking his paw. He must've stepped on a thorn, Billy thought. Then he was struck with another thought. Momma grizzly would think Billy was hurting her cub! Sure enough he turned just in time to see the bear tear out of the streambed, charging straight toward him.

Billy turned and ran down the trail as fast as he could. He remembered reading in a book that no man could outrun a bear, and what he needed to do was lay down in the trail and play dead. But in his terrified mind there was no way he could stop himself from running.

He tried to move as fast as he could but the light snow made the trail slippery. It was like he was in a bad dream trying to run through knee-deep molasses. His brain was telling his legs to move faster but his legs seemed unresponsive. He could hear the huge bear crashing through the bushes behind him. He could tell she was gaining on him.

He looked for a tree tall enough to climb up out of the bear's reach, but he could only see low-growing creek willows. He'd never be able to get high enough to escape the bear's razor-like claws. Billy's legs were tired and he was out of breath. He knew he was slowing down and he could tell that the bear was getting closer. Over the noise of his own breathing he could hear the bear's giant paws pounding the ground behind him. He could've sworn he felt the hot breath of the bear on his back.

Before he knew it, he was face first in the snow as he tripped over a root sticking up out of the ground and fell in a heap. He turned over and felt the pistol on his hip and remembered he was wearing Grandpa's gun belt. He grabbed the gun and held it out in front of him with both hands pointed at the giant bear, standing tall, roaring over him. He'd never been more terrified in his life. He tried to pull the trigger but it was stubborn and he needed both fingers to get the job done. He tugged hard and the trigger gave way. But instead of a loud bang there was only a quiet click. Billy pulled and pulled but the chambers were all empty. The gun wasn't even loaded! He lowered his gun, defeated by his own stupidity. Who grabs a gun and doesn't check for bullets? What was he thinking?

This was it. He was going to die. There was no way he could get up and run away fast enough. The bear gave another roar and put her front paws back on the ground. She crouched down and sniffed, prepared to lunge right at Billy. He closed his eyes and put his arms up over his face. Why did he ride out on his own? Why did he bring that stupid gun?

Suddenly a shot rang out. BANG! Then another. BANG! The report echoed across the valley. Billy opened his eyes to see the bear turn on her heels and lumber back up the trail. Her cub joined her and they lumbered back toward the woods. What had happened?

Billy turned to see Son sitting on Spirit, a wisp of smoke still seeping out of the end of the barrel of his rifle. Son continued to keep his rifle handy as he watched the momma bear and her cub work their way back across the river and up the trail on the other side. Only then did Son slip the rifle back into the holster underneath his stirrup and reach down to take Billy's hand.

"Come on Billy. Let's go home." Billy grabbed Son's hand and felt the strong pull up into the saddle behind his uncle. Billy wrapped his arms around Son's waist. He was never so happy to see someone in his life. He was stunned and his legs were like noodles hanging down from the saddle.

"Why didn't you shoot her Son? How did you know she'd spook and not attack me?"

"Sometimes," Son replied, "a warning shot is all you need. I figured all she wanted to do is protect her cub and she'd back off with just a shot in the sky. Besides a dead momma bear would've orphaned that little cub. You wouldn't want that would you?"

"Nope. I suppose not," Billy said.

"You know Billy, taking Grandpa's gun was a foolish thing to do. You could've seriously hurt yourself... or someone else."

"I know Son," Billy said. "I knew it was wrong, I just liked the way the gun felt. It made me feel like a real man. I thought I was ready to grow up a little bit more."

"Just because you carry a gun doesn't make you a man Billy. You can't rush growing up. There are things you just have to let happen in their own time. And you never take on something new without doing your homework first. You weren't ready for that responsibility and it almost cost you dearly. There will be time for you to learn how to handle that gun and when we have that lesson, we'll talk about checking to make sure it's loaded too."

"Sorry Son."

"That's okay Billy. You're forgiven. Have patience. I know it's frustrating but trying to take steps to grow up before you're ready isn't the answer. I'm just glad we were able to convince that momma bear not to pursue the matter any further!" Said Son through a big grin. "Let's find Blue and get that gun back where it belongs!"

Gradually, on the ride back to the farm, Billy's heartbeat returned to normal. He felt terrible about going off by himself and about taking the gun. He knew he was going to have to tell Grandpa but he was ready to admit his wrongdoing. Bit by bit, his fear and shame turned into courage and confidence. He knew he'd done wrong, but he felt a weight had been lifted by Son's forgiveness. He'd had an adventure! And he'd learned a valuable lesson. Now he would have a story of his own to tell some night after dinner.

CHAPTER EIGHT

Spring arrived on the farm in a rush. Flowers were blooming and trees were budding. The days were getting longer and the sunshine brighter. It was time to turn over the fallow soil and wake it up from its long winter nap. It was time to plant crops both at the farm and at the Indian village.

Billy and Son dragged the old rusty plow they got from Ned out of the barn. They took it apart and Son opened a drawer in the workbench and got out a rough whetstone. He showed it to Billy.

"This will help us to get that plow blade nice and sharp. I'll show you how this works. Hand me the plow blade." He took the blade from Billy and placed it in the vice mounted to the workbench. He snugged it down tight. "Now, you hold the stone in your hand like this," Son demonstrated, "and drag it across the blade. This'll put a new edge on that plow and help it to work just like new. Now you try."

Billy took the whetstone from Son and dragged it across the blade just like Son showed him. After several minutes of work, Billy felt his arm getting tired. Doing the same action with his arm over and over had caused the muscles in his arm to begin to ache. But instead of quitting or whining about how hard it was, the ache he felt only reminded him to pay close attention and make sure he did the job right.

Son noticed Billy's determination and smiled. "Billy, do you realize that it wasn't too long ago that you would've given up by now?" Billy looked up at Son and smiled.

Once the blade was sharp, Son showed Billy how to wipe it down with oil to keep it from rusting again. They fashioned new plow handles out of some lumber from a pile in the barn and attached them to the blade with new hardware. Lastly, they saddle-soaped the leather rigging that would harness Blue to the plow.

They sat back and looked at their handiwork. "That should do it," Son said.

"Wow, Son, this plow is almost like new!" Billy beamed. He was proud of the work they had accomplished together.

Billy's days were filled from dawn to dusk with hard work. But he loved it. He was doing work he felt was significant. No longer just feeding hogs on the farm, Billy was also able to help people and that made him feel like he was doing something important. Billy could feel himself changing. His thoughts were changing the way he acted and his actions were leading to some good habits in his life. He was beginning to see to the needs of others before his own and he saw even the difficult chores as steppingstones to something better. The days fell into a familiar routine with farm work in the early morning then riding to the Indian village a few times a week for more work before returning home in the dark, brushing the horses down before going in for a big dinner and stories in front of the wood stove.

But as the days passed Billy could sense a change coming over Son as well. He was becoming more and more quiet and seemed to be carrying a heavy load. Son had always cared a great deal about others but this was different. Even his shoulders appeared to sag under the weight. Billy couldn't put words to it but Son was turning inside himself...no longer joking around and laughing.

Billy first noticed the changes after their last trip to town. Not only was the hardware store off limits to them but now the grocery store and feed store had barred their doors as well. Billy and Son couldn't get their hair cut or mail a letter in town. People were closing their doors to them and the hostility they felt was harsh and personal.

What haunted Billy most was something Howard the barber said after closing his door to them. Billy and Son attempted to enter the barbershop to get a haircut only to be refused at the door. Getting a haircut with Son at Howard's shop had become a tradition. They got a trim most every time they came to town. Son would get a shave and even though Billy had only a few slow-growing whiskers, Howard would spread the warm lather on Billy's cheeks and shave them off with a flourish as if Billy had the thickest beard in town.

But this time Howard looked at them with such hatred. He said, "You won't get any service in this town Son. Don't think you can go out there and help those folks and then waltz back into town like it was nothing. That land out there is rightfully ours! We don't want those folks around and if you and Billy are going to continue to help them, we don't want you around either!"

"Why don't you like the Indians? What did they ever do to you?" Billy protested.

Howard took a breath, frustrated at having to explain to the young man. His arguments always felt weaker when uttered aloud.

"We heard about what a tribe of Indians done not a hunerd miles from here. Folks, peaceful folks mind you, were sleeping in their beds when those savages came in the night and burned their town to the ground. No call for it at all…just burned it to the ground."

"That's a shame," Son said.

"You bet it is!" interrupted Howard. "And let me tell you something else. You can bet that'll never happen in this town! Just shows you what bein' nice to Indians'll get you!"

Son held his hands up and shrugged his shoulders. "Now Howard, you know there's always two sides to every story. I'm not saying what those Indians did was right. But there's bound to be more to the story than meets the eye. I can also tell you that these Indians aren't like that. They only want to live in peace."

"Well, I don't trust 'em." Howard glared at Son and Billy. "And if you're siding with them, I don't trust you either!"

Those words continued to echo in Billy's heart as they left town that day. Riding in the wagon on the way home, Billy realized he wasn't angry toward the townspeople and he wasn't scared. He felt sorry for them. They weren't interested in hearing the truth about the Indians or about the mission to help them; their minds were made up. Billy felt sad for them.

Son spoke up and tore Billy away from his reverie. Son said that they'd have to rely more on Ned and the few other sympathetic folks in town to get what they needed. The work has to continue. It was more important now than ever before. Billy went to bed that night scared to think about what might happen in the future. But, he told himself, as long as Son was around everything would be okay.

Billy came downstairs for breakfast. It was warmer now and he no longer needed to dress in front of the stove. The mood in the house was somber with neither Grandpa nor Son talking much. They ate in silence and as Son took his last bite of eggs, he put his fork down with a heavy sigh. The day was just dawning but Son looked exhausted. He took his napkin, wiped his bushy mustaches and looked up.

"Tonight, I want to make dinner for you two. I want it to be special so I'll be in the kitchen most of the afternoon. Why don't you two knock off work a little early so you can get cleaned up before we eat. Let's plan on sitting down to dinner about sunset."

Billy and Grandpa looked at each other and then back at Son.

"Sure Son, if that's what you want," said Grandpa.

"Is there anything we can do to help?" said Billy

"Nope," Son said. He smiled but Billy could see the sadness in Son's eyes. He reached over to tussle Billy's hair, "Just stay out of the kitchen until dinner time. I want tonight to be a surprise." Billy and Grandpa agreed and they began their day.

They worked together all morning planting the first round of seeds in the garden. Billy cleaned out the barn and made the pigpen ready for the new batch of piglets they'd be getting soon. There was so much to do on the farm and the thought of all the additional work to do at the Indian village was overwhelming.

As the sun began to sink below the hilltop, Billy finished up his chores and headed inside to get washed up for dinner. As he went inside the back door, he could hear pots and pans banging around in the kitchen but after Son's warning, he didn't dare go in there. The smell coming from the kitchen was incredible and Billy couldn't wait to eat! After washing his face and hands, he headed up to change into his Sunday-best.

Dinner that night was unlike anything Billy had ever experienced. Not only had Son fixed dinner, he'd also set the table with china that only came out for special occasions. Son had even put fresh flowers in a vase in the center of the table.

Grandpa and Billy sat down to a big dinner of fried chicken, mashed potatoes, thick brown gravy, corn on the cob, green beans, a big fresh salad, cold iced tea and a big slab of cinnamon apple pie. They talked and laughed and for a while it seemed that Son was his old self again. They told stories about their work and laughed about the funny things that had happened. Billy told Grandpa about Ned and his crazy dogs. It was hard to finish the meal they were laughing so much. Gradually the subject turned to the future and what would happen in the coming months.

They outlined plans for the future, both at the farm and at the Indian village. They would have to check with Ned about more supplies. Ned told them about others in town who were sympathetic to the cause and wanted to help. Many were skittish and afraid of being seen around town with Son, so they painted a small red hand on the doorposts of their homes. That way, Son and Billy would know who they could count on.

Seconds were served while Son told of other villages that needed help. He pulled out the little book from his front shirt pocket and carefully opened it to the pages marked with the red scarlet ribbon. Billy could barely make out the words "The Mission" in faded gold foil stamped on the cover. Son flipped to the back of the book and ran his calloused finger down the page. Billy could see the careful script where Son had recorded details about the various people he had helped. He could see where Son had sketched maps and directions of where to find these people.

Son looked up from the book. He turned to Billy and said, "Over the last couple of years I've kept this journal. It's just my own scratching really. Thoughts about the people I've met and the things I've done..." His voice trailed off.

"But Billy, I've written ideas here too. There's so much more to do, so many more to help. That's in here too. The things I *want* to do." His voice broke with emotion. In that moment, Billy would've given his right arm to do whatever it took to help Son with his mission.

They talked long after the last bit of pie was eaten. When the conversation waned, Son took his napkin and wiped off his mouth and took a deep solemn breath. He looked at Grandpa and Billy and said, "I made this dinner for a reason. I'm going away and from now on, every time you eat fried chicken or apple pie, I want you to remember this night and the work we've done together. I want you to remember the stories and the meals and the rides and the conversations we've had. Whenever you eat a meal like this, I want you to recommit yourself to the work of helping others and continuing the work we've started."

Wait a minute! Billy was confused. Going away? He thought Son would stay on the farm with them forever! How could the work continue if Son left them? He had so many questions and the troubled words rushed out of his mouth all at once. He was gripped by that old familiar fear of being left behind. It was like watching your family pull away in the wagon without you. Grandpa put his big hand on Billy's shoulder and squeezed. Son said, "It'll all be okay Billy. You'll see."

But it was not okay. Why was Son acting so strange? Why did he have to leave? Billy thought Son was getting him ready for some great mission. Billy imagined working the rest of his life alongside Son. But now Son was taking that dream away from him. He was going to be stuck on this farm for the rest of his life! He'd never be a cowboy!

Billy threw his napkin on the table and ran upstairs and fell on his bed. He was angry and hurt and scared. Things had been going so well. Why did everything have to change? He tried to calm down and convince himself that Son's final words were true, that it would be okay. But it was no use. He knew that it would not be okay. He knew that everything would be different and that he'd be left alone once again, just like when his parents left him. He buried his face in the pillow to muffle his sobbing. He didn't want anyone to hear him crying. He wept until sleep overcame him.

CHAPTER NINE

Billy awoke with the pain of last night still lingering in his heart. He stared at the ceiling of his bedroom where the early sunlight cast shadows as it shone through the lace curtains. He looked around his room and saw the pictures on the wall, the furniture, his clothes tossed in the corner on the chair. Everything was familiar but seemed flat as if someone had let the air out. Billy could feel the shift.

His eyes continued to scan across the familiar room. He looked at his small desk in front of the window. He saw the oil lamp, the mirror, his comb, the knife that Son gave him and a few other things he normally kept in his pants pockets. But what caught Billy's eye was something new he'd never seen on the desk before. He got up to take a closer look.

Leaning up against the oil lamp was a letter. Billy picked up the thick paper envelope and recognized

Son's flowing script. Written boldly on the envelope was the name, "William Adam Christian." Billy hadn't thought of his full name in years. He didn't know Son was even aware of what his full name was. He turned the envelope over and found it sealed with bright red wax; the letters "SC" stamped into it.

Billy quickly broke the seal, opened the letter and began to read.

> *My Dear Boy,*
>
> *From the first day I saw you sitting on that fence watching those hungry hogs, I knew we'd be friends, brothers.*
>
> *You remind me of myself: energetic, inquisitive and curious about your world, always willing to help someone in need.*
>
> *You've learned a lot, Billy and I couldn't be more proud. I believe with all my heart that you're ready to take over my work.*
>
> *I see all the best of your father in you Billy. I know he made some big mistakes but the best of him is in you. You have his strength and courage. And you have his strong will. These qualities will serve you well as you grow into the man you were born to be.*

Billy paused and looked out the window in front of him. Tears began to well up in his eyes. He looked back down and continued to read.

> *By the time you read this, I'll be gone. But never forget who you are and the things I've taught you. Never forget how important your thoughts are. Remember they are the foundation of your actions and your actions become your habits. And your habits will lead you to the thing you want most of all. They lead you to do the things you were born to do. And that, my William, is your Destiny.*
>
> *Never be afraid to try new things or go to new places. There's always an adventure over the next hill. Wherever your adventures lead you, I'll be by your side. Always. I wish you the best and Godspeed,*

At the bottom of the page Billy recognized the capital initial S that Son had signed with a flourish.

Billy lay the pages down on the desk and noticed something else. He reached in the envelope and pulled out a small journal. It was the book that Son always carried! The book fit easily in his hand. It was old and weathered and held together by a length of twine wrapped around its width. The narrow spine was a faded red and on the black leather cover was stamped in foil, "The Mission." Billy couldn't believe it. He was holding Son's book!

He opened it and began to flip through the pages. He recognized Son's fine handwriting and was intrigued by the drawings. He saw maps and charts and even a page of strange symbols drawn, along with their meanings.

He got dressed, grabbed the letter and book off the desk and shoved them deep in his back pocket as he ran downstairs. An eerie stillness met him. He sensed a change in the air, an emptiness that left a giant hole—like someone had reached inside and ripped out his heart.

He could hear someone in the kitchen and went in to find Grandpa. He was frying some bacon and eggs for breakfast. The chair where Son normally sat in the mornings was empty. Billy choked back tears and cleared his throat.

"Do you know where Son went?" Billy stammered.

Without looking up Grandpa said, "Men from town came to get him early this morning…a couple of hours ago. They said they were taking him back to town to stand trial."

"Trial? What did he do that was so wrong?" Billy cried.

"Billy," Grandpa turned to look at his grandson. "Son knew this was going to happen. He was ready and went with them without a fuss. The folks in town never have understood the work you two have been doing in the village. They're scared and they're lashing out. Change is hard, especially when they feel it's out of their control. You know how that feels. You want to do anything you can to get things back to the way they used to be. The folks in town figure if they can just get Son to stop his work, they can go back to living the way they want."

Billy shook his head. "But I helped Son. Why didn't they get me too?"

"They said you're young and impressionable. They think the real threat is Son and his influence over you and others."

Billy sagged into Son's kitchen chair. He was dazed and defeated. But he knew he had to find Son. Maybe he could explain. Suddenly inspired, he went to the back door without a word and put on his coat and hat. He strode purposefully to the barn and saddled up Blue for the ride to town. He climbed up and nudged Blue out of the barn and down the driveway. He started off at a trot but the longer he rode, the more urgency he felt. He reached up and pulled his hat down tight on his head and spurred Blue into a full gallop. They turned the last bend, crossed the bridge and rode full speed into town not even noticing the people eyeing him. He pulled up in front of the sheriff's office and jumped off Blue, barely taking the time to tie her to the hitching post. He ran up the steps and burst in the door yelling, "What have you done with Son!"

CHAPTER TEN

The sheriff and two deputies huddled deep in cahoots around a small desk but jerked up when they heard the commotion coming through the front door.

The sheriff stood up to his full height and put his thumbs in his belt. The two dull-witted deputies leaned back in their chairs, relishing their front-row seats. They glanced at one another and a stupid grin passed between them exposing their few stained teeth. This counted as the best entertainment they'd had in months.

The sheriff eyed Billy up and down, leaned over and spit a perfect bull's-eye in the nearby spittoon. He held his hands out open in front of him and smirked, "Now settle down boy. We've got your uncle locked up and there's nothing you're going to do about it. He ain't getting out of here anytime soon.

He has to wait to see the judge for trial. The judge won't even be here for another week or so. If you want to see him, I'll take you back but you're gonna have to simmer down. I won't tolerate a scene."

Billy felt the impulse to draw his knife and rush the sheriff but fought it back. The thought of Son being held captive was more than he could bear but he knew this wasn't the time to be rash. He took a deep breath and found his self-control. He dug his fingernails into his palms, bit his lip and looked the sheriff straight in the eye.

The sheriff motioned to a thick wooden door and said, "Your uncle's back here."

The sheriff reached up high on the wall and grabbed a ring of giant keys, "Follow me," he said. Under the deputies' watchful eyes, the sheriff led Billy through the door and down the long hallway. There were no windows or lights and Billy could barely make out the sheriff walking just in front of him. At the end of the hall the sheriff picked out a different key and put it in the lock of another thick wooden door. The lock gave way and the sheriff slid the bolt and opened the massive door with a loud creak.

Billy followed him through the door and into another dark hallway. The only light came from a tiny barred window at the end of the narrow passage, the morning sun's pale shaft hardly making a dent in the darkness. The air was dank and musty, thick with the desperation and fear of men in trouble.

This hallway was different than the first with three small jail cells running down the left side. The bars were thick and solid. Billy clung to the wall on his right as he edged down the hallway wanting to keep as much distance between himself and the bars as he could. When the sheriff passed the first cell door the prisoner yelled out, "When are we gonna get some grub in here? We're starving!" He banged his tin cup on the bars.

"Shut up! You'll eat when I get hungry!" yelled the Sheriff.

Billy could hear more loud complaints coming from down the hall in the last cell but he stopped in front of the cell in the middle. In the shadows, he saw Son on his knees at the edge of the thin cell bunk. He had his head bent down with his hands clasped in front of him. Billy stopped and stared with his mouth open. He barely recognized his uncle.

Son was still in his nightshirt, wearing his trousers but no belt or suspenders. He was dirty and barefoot and his hair was matted with dried blood. Without his hat or his boots, he looked as if he'd shrunk in size. Son slowly stood and turned to face Billy. His shoulders sagged and Billy noticed one of his eyes was swollen almost shut. Billy was shocked to see the sadness in Son's face. A wave of despair hit Billy, drowning him in darkness. He felt like he was going to faint. He reached out, grabbed the bars of the cell door and sunk down to his knees. His cheeks flushed red and he knew he was about to cry but he didn't care.

Son moved to the cell door and grabbed Billy's hands through the bars. He bent down to look Billy in the face. Through his thick mustaches, he smiled a sad smile and awkwardly tried to give Billy a hug through the thick iron bars. The sheriff looked on but he was a hard man and the powerful emotions in the cramped space made him uncomfortable. With disgust, he left the two alone and walked back down the long hallway through the big door and back to his office.

After the sheriff closed the door, Billy whispered "What's happening Son? Why are you here?"

The prisoners on each side were making a racket and Son had to work hard to hear his nephew. He leaned closer and said, "The folks here in town have filed charges against me for helping the Indians. There's a law on the books that prohibits anyone without proper governmental authorization and certification from helping any Indians."

"But what's going to happen to you? You've done nothing wrong!"

"I'm waiting now to go to trial."

"But all you're trying to do is help those people!"

"And that's the very thing they have a problem with Billy." He reached through the bars and took Billy's quivering chin and held his face close. "Remember what I told you about how people have a tough time when changes come? These folks are scared and they're doing what seems right to them. Fear has blinded them and they don't know what they're doing."

Billy realized for the first time that Son was carrying a burden for the townspeople just like he did for the Indians. Even now, stuck in jail, with a hangman's noose threating his life, he was thinking of others.

"Billy, I don't want you to worry about what's going to happen. I need you to be brave and do something for me. Get back to the farm as soon as you can. Pack the saddlebags, and ride out to the Indian village, and do it quickly. With me out of the way, the folks here in town are emboldened to act out against the Indians. You've got to warn them that they have to leave the valley and head west. I need you to stay and help them prepare for their long journey."

Billy shook his head, confused.

Son lowered his voice and moved in closer, "Billy, look. I'm not the only one that these folks want to get. I overheard the sheriff talking to his deputies about getting up a group of folks and riding out and capturing the chief and elders of the tribe. The Indians were forced by the government to live out there in the valley. But now, these folks in town have it in their minds to grab that land. They want the Indians gone, and the sooner the better. Their plan is to arrest the leaders and put them on trial with me. Then they aim to burn the village to the ground. Those folks will be without their leaders and without a place to live. I know they'll try to fight back but there's no way they'll survive. The townsfolk are determined to take that land. You've got to ride out there and warn them!"

Billy's mouth dropped open. "I can't do that! I can't go by myself! I need you to go with me!" Billy grabbed the thick bars and tried to shake them loose. "Let's see if there's a way to get you out of here. Maybe we can get a lawyer! Maybe me and Grandpa can come back tonight and bust you out!"

"No, Billy. I'm doing exactly what I need to be doing right now. This is my journey. But you've got a journey of your own, one you've got to take without me."

Son leaned toward Billy, "Do you have the book I left on your desk?"

"What're you two mumblin' about?" Shouted one of the prisoners.

"Nothing that concerns you, my friend." The sudden steady strength in Son's voice surprised Billy.

Son turned back to Billy, "Do you have the book?"

Billy nodded. "Good, keep that book with you always. It'll help you. It's a record of the work I've been doing. Let it be your guide. I want you to write down the work you do in the book as well. That way others will know and it'll help them someday. Do you understand?"

Billy nodded again. There was so much to remember. This was crazy! Billy shook his head, trying to clear his thoughts.

"But what about the plowing and planting that still need to be done out there?" asked Billy.

"That doesn't matter now, Billy. Those folks have to get out of that valley and you're going to have to lead them."

Son took a deep breath. He looked down, trying to remember everything he wanted to tell the boy. "And one more thing. I want you to take Spirit. He's your horse now. He'll know what to do."

"But I can't ride Spirit! He's too much horse for me. You said so yourself!"

"I've been training you for this very moment Billy! You've learned so much and done so well. You've grown. You're no longer a farm boy; you're a strong young man. I know you can ride Spirit. This is your time. Remember all your dreams? This is the time for those dreams to come true! Will you do this for me?"

Billy steeled himself and said, "Yes, Son. But I don't mind telling you, I'm pretty nervous about all this."

Son smiled. "It's okay to be nervous. I know you can do this. Now, there's something else I want you to do. I want you to wear my duster and hat. They're hanging in the house by the back door."

"But your things are too big for me! I can't wear them!"

Son grabbed Billy's shoulders through the bars of the jail cell door. "You have to trust me Billy. You've grown more than you know. Now get back to the farm. Grab some food from the kitchen and some extra clothes. Pack the saddlebags; you'll be gone for a while. Put on the hat and duster, then get on Spirit and get out there to the village as soon as you can. You can do this. You've got to hurry and warn those people. Now RIDE!"

CHAPTER ELEVEN

Billy ran back down the narrow hallway in a daze. He banged on the thick wooden door for the sheriff to come let him out. After a moment he heard the key clatter in the lock and the door opened with a loud creak. Without a word he passed the sheriff, ignoring the stares of the deputies. He ran through the office and out the door. He untied Blue from the rail and climbed up on her back. He hurried back to the farm, his mind still whirling with so many unanswered questions.

He rode up the drive and into the barn, quickly taking the tack off of Blue and giving her some hay in her stall. He went to the back of the barn to grab the saddlebags. Spirit turned his head to look at Billy and lowed deeply. It's like he knew something was up. Billy couldn't bring himself to look at Spirit right now. He was too uncertain to think about what he had to do next.

He went inside and found Grandpa sitting at his desk in the front parlor. Billy sat down in the side chair and told his Grandpa the whole story, all about the sheriff, Son in the jail cell, and the new mission.

"He wants me to continue his work Grandpa. He's not coming back."

"I know." Grandpa picked up a piece of paper from his desk and showed it to Billy.

Billy looked at his Grandpa curiously. "You think you're the only one who got a letter from Son?" Billy took the opened letter and quickly scanned it. It was similar to the one he had gotten from Son.

"I've got to go Grandpa. I've got to get out to the village and warn the people."

Grandpa nodded. "I've got a few things packed for you to eat. They're on the kitchen counter, ready to go in the saddlebag."

Billy ran upstairs and threw some clothes in one of the saddlebags. He folded Son's letter and put it in his pocket along with the book. He went back downstairs to the kitchen, grabbed the food and went to say good-bye to his grandpa.

Grandpa stood up at his desk where he'd been working and opened his arms as Billy came into the parlor. Billy melted into Grandpa's chest and felt his big, strong arms fold around him, holding him close. He felt Grandpa's scratchy whiskers on his forehead and smelled the coffee aroma still clinging to his soft flannel shirt.

"Good-bye Grandpa. I love you."

"Good-bye William."

Billy pulled back and looked at Grandpa. He'd never heard Grandpa call him that name. "William?" Billy asked.

"Yeah, you've grown. You're not Billy anymore. It's time your name fit the young man you've become."

"But I'm scared Grandpa. I don't know where to go or what to do."

Grandpa smiled at the scared young man before him.

"William. My Will. What did Son tell you to do?"

"He said to go to the Indian village and warn them about the townspeople and then to continue his work. But I'm not sure what that means. How will I know where to go? How will I find food to eat? How will I earn the money to live?"

Grandpa smiled as he took Billy's face in his hands and looked deep in his eyes. "You'll be just fine. Just take it one thing at a time. Son wouldn't have trusted you with this if he didn't think you could handle it." Grandpa reached down and grabbed something out of the bottom drawer of his roll-top desk. He smiled as he handed the gun belt and Colt revolver to Billy. Billy took them and looked up curiously at his Grandpa.

Grandpa said, "You'll need this more than I will. Take it." Then he remembered something else and reached back into the drawer and grabbed a box of bullets. "And don't forget the bullets." They shared a knowing smile. Billy put the gun belt around his waist and buckled it, before reaching for the box. Billy gave his Grandpa one last big hug. He knew he had to go but didn't want to leave the warmth of his Grandpa's embrace. He finally pulled away and wiped the tears away from his face.

With one last look over his shoulder, Billy made his way through the kitchen toward the back door. He looked up on the wall to see Son's duster and hat hanging on their pegs. He put the saddlebags on the floor and reached up to take the duster down and put it on. Tentatively, he put his arms in the sleeves knowing the coat would be way too big.

As he shrugged on the duster something strange happened. The coat fit like it was made just for him. It didn't feel heavy or cumbersome. It rested lightly on his shoulders. He stretched his hands out in front of him to find that the sleeves reached perfectly to his wrists and when he buttoned it up it fit around him snuggly just the way it was supposed to. He moved his arms to find that the coat didn't tug or pull but moved with him, just like a second skin.

He looked inside the left side of the coat. There embroidered over the inside pocket was his name, "William Adam Christian." He reached into the pocket and felt something. It felt like a piece of cloth, a rag. But when he pulled it out he noticed that it wasn't just a rag. It was a faded cloth with symbols stitched on it. It was stained with blood. This was the cloth that Red Buffalo had given Son, the one he had wrapped his hand in after he cut it with the knife! He almost started to cry but braced himself and put the cloth back in his duster pocket.

He reached up for the hat and put it on expecting it to fall down over his ears and eyes. But as the hat came down on the top of his head, he could feel the hatband tighten around his forehead. He pulled it down until it fit just over his eyes. He noticed the reflection of himself in the small mirror by the door. He saw a Billy he'd not seen before. With Son's hat and coat on, he looked older and wiser. Now he saw William. As he searched his face in the mirror, he quietly whispered, "Am I Will?"

As he said it he felt something deep in his chest begin to rise, something sleepy now coming awake. He looked down at his hands and noticed that they were a man's hands. He felt the strength in his arms and the power in his back. He thought about the boy he'd been and the man he was becoming. He still didn't know exactly what he was going to do, but now he knew exactly who he was. He looked at the mirror again and said to himself with resolve, "I AM WILL."

,He realized he was no longer scared. He didn't know the whole picture, but he knew the next step: Go get Spirit and go to the village. And for now, that was enough. He knew the rest would work out. With his newly found confidence he bent to get the sad-dlebags off the floor and slung them over his broad shoulder. Then he reached for the squeaky screen door, pulled it open and went out to the barn.

CHAPTER TWELVE

As Will walked to the barn he was amazed at how the duster and hat fit him. In fact, they fit so well he could barely feel he was wearing them at all. He knew he looked different on the outside and now he realized that he felt different on the inside too. With the duster and hat on, he felt like he was "wearing" Son. He carried himself differently. He viewed himself with different eyes and thought of himself in different terms. He wasn't the farm boy Billy anymore. He was Will now. He had a mission to fulfill and like Son had taught him, there's nothing more dangerous to the enemy than a man with a mission.

He reached out and slid open the heavy barn door. The sunlight shone through the gaps between the boards; hay dust floated in the beams of light. From the shadows he could make out the two horses in their stalls. Blue was busy eating, her head buried in the trough, but Spirit was alert with his ears pointed forward, watching Will.

As Will approached, he had the courage to look into the eyes of Spirit. He spoke quietly, trying to reassure the horse. "Hey, there boy. It's okay. We've got a job to do. Are you up for a ride?"

Spirit lowed a quiet response. Will could sense the giant horse knew exactly what was going on and what needed to happen. He entered Spirit's stall and began to get him ready for the long ride ahead. Spirit lowered his head so Will could easily slip the bridle over his ears. He worked the bit into Spirit's mouth. He placed the saddle blanket on Spirit's back and noticed for the first time the strange symbols embroidered on the blanket. These were similar to the symbols on the bloodstained cloth in his pocket. Where had he seen those symbols before? ,In Son's book! Yes, he'd seen those same symbols in Son's small book.

He looked again at the blanket. There were four symbols in all, stitched across the lower edge as it was draped over Spirit's back. The first symbol, on the left, was a circle with five vertical lines drawn over the top of the circle. To the right of the circle was the next symbol, a handprint. Next came another hand-print but with a plus sign in the middle of the palm of the hand. Finally, on the right was a crooked arrow drawn, pointing to the right.

Will reached into his pants pocket and pulled out the book. He flipped back to the pages where the symbols were drawn and their meanings were listed. First, the circle with the lines over it. He ran his finger down the left side of the page until he found the small symbol. Then he moved his finger to the right to find the meaning, "Thoughts."

He found the second symbol, the handprint, and its meaning, "Actions." Then the palm with the plus sign, "Habits." Finally the crooked right arrow, "Destiny." Will recognized the saying. *"Thoughts lead to Actions, which lead to Habits, which lead to your Destiny."* Will couldn't help smiling. His uncle's valuable lessons had been embroidered right in front of him this whole time and he'd never noticed. Will remembered Son's words, "The small things we do every day are important. They lead to the habits that form our ultimate Destiny." He remembered Son telling him about each day, each task, becoming the building blocks of the life he wanted. He knew he was about to step into that life.

He closed the book and put it back in his pocket. He reached for the giant saddle and was surprised at how light it was as he lifted it onto the horse's back. He noticed that there were many more symbols stamped in the leather of the saddle. There was no time to translate them all right now. He would have to do that later. He made sure the stirrups hung straight and then grabbed the latigo strap and fed it through the cinch loop and pulled it up tight, just like Son taught him.

He threw the saddlebags on the back of the saddle and tucked them under the bedroll. He even took Son's rifle and slid it into its holster under the left stirrup and tucked a full box of cartridges deep in the saddlebag. He was ready. He reached up for the horn and placed his foot in the stirrup and swung his leg over the back of the horse. He settled himself into the saddle and grabbed the reins. They were worn smooth and felt supple in his hands. Spirit glanced back at his new rider.

Will returned the gaze. He was actually up on Spirit! He touched his heels to Spirit's ribs and they slowly rode out of the barn. As they emerged into the sunlight, Will reached up and pulled the hat snug down on his head. He clicked his tongue and Spirit started off in a trot down the driveway. They crossed the river and then in a full gallop they left the valley and rode up into the hills toward the Indian village.

CHAPTER THIRTEEN

A s Will rode the trail with Spirit, he felt that Son was with him every step of the way. Through the wind in the pines he could hear Son's voice encouraging him and urging him onward. Spirit ran the trail with purpose and Will could feel the horse's power beneath him. He stood in the stirrups and held the reins tightly in his left hand. They moved as one down the backside of the hill and into the valley below.

They stopped at the river for a drink but then continued their ride through the woods. Spirit barely slowed as they climbed higher and higher into the hills. As Spirit navigated the trail, Will's mind began to wander to the village and what he might find when he got there. He rehearsed what he was going to say. Could he communicate in their language? Could he make them understand what they had to do?

They crested the last hill and looked down on the village. He remembered the first time he came to this village with Son. He remembered meeting the Indians and playing with the children while Son discussed important matters with the elders. He remembered his own first introduction to the council of elders. But now there was no time to play with the children and there was no Son to take the lead with the elders. Will was going to have to be the one to speak to the council. He would have to convince them to leave and leave quickly.

Will rode into the village. At first, the villagers thought he was Son. But when he got closer they saw that it was Will and immediately knew something was wrong. He rode to the center of the village and climbed down off Spirit. One of the older boys ran up and took the leather reins and led Spirit away to get some water as Will mustered his courage to speak with the elders.

When he bent down to enter the lodge he could feel the embrace of the duster around his ribs. He knew Son was with him. He stepped inside, stood up tall and gave himself a moment for his eyes to adjust to the dim and smoky space. There was a low fire burning in the center and men smoking their pipes, sitting in a circle around the edges of the lodge. They were speaking together in small groups. It was clear that Will had interrupted an important council meeting.

The men stopped talking and looked up. Will took off his hat as one of the elders made a place on the bearskin for him. The elders could tell something was different. Will had never come to the village without Son and they had never seen Will wearing the duster or hat. They leaned forward and waited.

Will spoke to the men in their own language, haltingly at first. Although he'd learned quite a bit over the past months, he'd only spoken to the children, and even then he'd only spoken when he needed to. Occasionally Son would help him but now with such an important message to give, Will felt the pressure to get the words just right.

The more he spoke, the easier it became. He could hear the words in his head first and then he spoke them aloud. He shared the news about Son and the townspeople. The elders erupted in anger and began shouting all at once. Will hadn't even gotten to the part about having to leave the valley!

Chief Red Buffalo raised his hands and called them to order. He told the elders that they must form a war party and burn the town to the ground!

"We must strike first before they can attack us!" It was as if all the pent up anger was boiling over in the council meeting.

"We must have our revenge!"

The men began to beat their drums and shout— each trying to be heard over the other. Will stood up. "NO!" But he didn't stand a chance of being heard above the din.

Will remembered this was just the scenario Son predicted. He had to stop them. What could he do to make them listen? Then he remembered the blood-stained cloth! He reached into his duster pocket and took out the cloth. He held it out in his hand.

"STOP!"

A hush fell over the group. The elders looked up at Will, shocked that the young outsider would dare raise his voice to the council.

"That's not what Son wanted!" Will exclaimed. "This cloth is a symbol of Son's love for your people. He loves you and only wants what's best for you. This cloth is proof of that!"

He continued, "Son told me that you must not go to town. He's instructed me to tell you not to worry about him but to help you get ready to leave the village. The men from town are riding out to arrest the council to stand trial with Son. Then they will attack the village. We have no choice but to leave the valley. There's no time to waste!"

The elders erupted in shouting. They were all trying to talk at once. Will had trouble making out everything they were saying but from what he could tell, most of the men still wanted to attack, to raid them before they had a chance to organize an attack of their own.

"NO!" Will shouted again. "Attacking them will only make things worse! They have far more resources than we do. We would be defeated if we tried to attack them." But the council wasn't listening. Their anger was growing and their shouts became louder and more intense.

Will looked across the circle at Chief Red Buffalo. He held the cloth out toward the chief one last time and looked him squarely in the eye. The chief nodded his head. He understood.

The elders continued their shouting but Red Buffalo called them to order. He reached down to his waist and pulled a matching bloodstained cloth from the belt Son had given him. He held the cloth up to the council and looked at Will. He said, "This young man is right. This is a symbol of our brotherhood with Son. He trusts this young man and we must as well. We must honor his wisdom and do as his nephew says. This is not the time to fight. We must prepare to leave the valley. Go to your families. Make preparations to leave at once!

The elders may have had other opinions but the debate was over. They got up without another word. The chief had spoken and the matter was settled. They made their way out of the council lodge to prepare to leave the valley.

CHAPTER FOURTEEN

Will was amazed as he watched the village being dismantled, packed up and loaded onto the Indian ponies for travel. With no wagons, the Indians devised a simple solution for hauling their gear over long distances using the same materials their tepees were made out of.

First the women took the tepees down and laid the skins and poles on the ground in neat stacks. Will stopped what he was doing to help and looked on as the men took the poles and laid them on each side of the ponies, pointing the narrow ends of the poles toward the front. Then they picked up the narrow ends of each pole and lashed them to the sides of the pony forming a giant letter "A" with the pony standing in the middle. Next they took skins from the lodges and stretched them between the larger ends of the poles behind the pony. They called this a travois and it allowed the ponies to carry much more than if they just stacked their bundles on the ponies' backs. The women began to load their belongings on the skins. The small children climbed on top of the load to ride.

As the people worked, they sang. It was a sad but beautiful song. As Will leaned in to listen, the words of the mournful song came to him on the gentle breeze...

Our fathers in the days of old
Walked soft upon the earth and told
Of how to live and how to hold
The rivers and the streams with water cold
As a diamond, jewel or precious gold

Forced to flee the place they knew
The land of the maple and the spruce
The hunting ground of bear and moose
A land of love and peace to lose
To wander the earth, not ours but whose?

As our fathers sat at council fires
Thoughts of ancients on the pyres
Cut their hands against the liars
With shoulders back and heads held higher
Never again to live so dire

This is our life, our sacred vow
Ne'er to bend with heads a-bow
We'll stand with pride for what is ours
Prepared to fight and not to cower
It is our headright, our holy dower

And now as sons we wander alone
Far from the land that we have known
Far from the fields that we have sown
Into a place that's not our own
We search for a place to call our home

Their voices lilted above the valley floor like smoke rising from cook fires as they packed up the pieces of their lives and made ready to leave. Once again they were forced to move, to uproot their lives and find a new place to call home.

Once their belongings were ready for travel, the people restored the land to its original beauty. They took up the fencing they'd just run and scattered the rocks they had used as boundaries and fire circles and even used tumbleweeds to sweep the area clean of debris. When the land was clean and they were ready to move out, Red Buffalo bent over and gathered a handful of dried sage in his fist. He twisted the sage together into a smudge and lit the end of it from the lone remaining fire. As the smudge began to smoke, he held it up in his hand and began to circle it over his head. He sang a sacred prayer to cleanse and bless the land. He made a small stack of stones and poured water over the stack and remaining embers. He bowed deeply. Once he was finished, the tribe mounted up and began the ride up and out of the valley. Will noticed that no one turned to look back.

They fell into an uneven single-file line, some walking, some on horseback, a few leading horses laden with supplies, and still others leading the young children.

After a long day on the trail, they stopped for the night as the sun was beginning to set. Will had ridden ahead and found a perfect spot that allowed the people shelter among the trees but also afforded them views in all directions. They untied the litters from the ponies and gave them some hay. They gathered firewood and built small cook fires to prepare something to eat. They unpacked and laid out skins to cover the ground. They would move out in the morning at first light so they would just unload enough here for their overnight stay.

Will was troubled. These people trusted him to lead them to a new place they could call home but he didn't know where he was going. Spirit seemed to be able to pick out a path through the wilderness but Will remained confused. The people trusted Red Buffalo. Red Buffalo trusted Will. But Will wasn't so sure he trusted himself.

As the people were making ready for the night, Will slipped away to a secluded spot along the ridge where he could watch the sunset. His mind was reeling. In the distance he noticed three giant pine trees growing alone in a straight row way out on the horizon. They looked like soldiers standing at attention, guarding the valley below.

Absent-mindedly, he began complaining to himself about his situation; he wrestled with his thoughts trying to keep them under control. What was he doing? How in the world did he think he was going to pull this "rescue" off without Son? He felt almost silly wearing the coat and hat, like a kid pretending to be someone he wasn't. But with newfound resolve, he closed his eyes and stopped the flow of negative thoughts. He took a deep breath and stilled himself.

Before he knew it, he was talking to Son. He told Son about the village and about the mass exodus. He explained how the people trusted him but that he didn't even know where to go. He hadn't been this far away from home before. He wasn't even sure where they were. He was overwhelmed with the unknown that yawned out in front of him.

As Will unloaded his heart to Son, he heard a small voice deep inside his heart. The voice simply said, "Look in the book. The answer is in the book."

Of course! Son's book! Will remembered seeing hand-drawn maps in the book! Will reached into his pocket and pulled out the old leather journal. He thumbed through the pages without really know-ing what he was looking for. He came to a section of pages with maps drawn on them. Something caught his eye as he flipped through the pages. He went back. There! In the upper left corner of the page, Son had drawn three trees in a row. Underneath the trees he'd written, "The Three Sentries." Now he knew where he was! Now he had a map!

He looked closer and with red ink, Son had scrawled a trail on this map from the Three Sentries in the upper left corner to a place in the lower right of the map called "Indian Territories." The line went through forests, over hills and across rivers. Will wasn't exactly sure what the Indian Territories were but he sensed that this was their new destination. Son had answered him! Son directed him to the book and now they had Son's red line to follow!

CHAPTER FIFTEEN

Their journey stretched on. Days turned into weeks. Along the trail of the thin red line, babies were born and many of the older folks passed away. Each day the people would rise with the sun, pack up their belongings, put out their cook fires and begin the new day's travel. Will and Spirit led them, carefully following Son's map, checking off landmarks along the way.

The trail was difficult but they had food to eat, water to drink and fair weather to travel by. They no longer posted guards at night. It seemed that leaving the valley was enough for the townspeople who had long since given up the chase. After months of hard travel over rough terrain, the small band of Indians arrived at their destination, the Indian Territories.

They camped along a broad slow-moving river, just outside a small town with a strange name, Tahlequah, the capital town of the Cherokee Nation. Will and Red Buffalo left the tribe and crossed the river at the ford.

Riding side by side into town, they each felt this place was different. There were just as many Indians here as there were white folks. There didn't seem to be the tension and unrest here. People, both Indian and white, greeted each other as they passed on the wooden sidewalks and dirt streets.

Will looked over at Red Buffalo, riding tall and proud. He had put on his headdress for the ride to town and he looked magnificent; the feathers of his ceremonial crown shone in the sunlight as they rode down the main street. After so much time on the trail, Will sure hoped this would be the new home for his friends.

Will looked to his right and caught the eyes of a young man carrying a sack of seed over his shoulder along the raised wooden sidewalk. Will called out, "Who's in charge around here?"

After a quick glance at Red Buffalo the young man looked over at Will and said, "You'll want to talk to one of the agents. They should be in their office. It's just down that way, next to the bank," he said pointing down the street. "They should be able to answer any questions."

"Thank you kindly," Will said as he tipped his hat.

They found the agent's office on the main street, between the Mercantile and the bank, just where the young man said it would be. They looked up at a brightly painted sign, "CHEROKEE INDIAN NATION – AGENT'S OFFICE."

They pulled their horses up to the hitching rail under the sign and climbed down. They went up the steps and stood at the office door. Will put his hand on the doorknob and felt the butterflies in his stomach. "I'm nervous," he thought. He heard Son's immediate reply in his heart, "It's okay to be nervous." Will smiled to himself. Son must've said that to him hundreds of times.

Will took a deep breath, looked over at Red Buffalo and nodded. He turned the knob and they walked in together. They entered into a large room with high ceilings and a high counter along the back. The room was crowded with people who were hot and dusty. It was a warm midsummer day and the air in the office was stuffy. Sitting behind the counter were four men, each with a large leather ledger on the counter in front of them. There were lines of people waiting in front of each man. It appeared that this is where the people must register before settling.

Will and Red Buffalo picked the shortest line and began the wait to talk to an agent. Finally, they made their way to the counter where a small nameplate was mounted. In bold letters it read, "HARPER." Mr. Harper sat behind the counter in front of them. He was a small man with an ill-fitting navy blue uniform with brass buttons that went all the way up to his collar. Will thought this man was probably just as stuffy as the room. Mr. Harper had narrow shoulders and greasy hair combed over a large bald spot on the top of his head. His skin was pale and moist from sweat and he wore a small pair of wire-framed glasses down on his nose. His voice was high-pitched and squeaky as he raised his head and called out, "Next!"

Will explained their situation and introduced Red Buffalo. Will translated between the two as Mr. Harper had many questions for Red Buffalo about his people. As he stood there, Will realized that he had judged too quickly. Mr. Harper was patient and kind and he spoke warmly to Red Buffalo. With a shaky hand, Mr. Harper dipped his pen in the ink well and began to take down the information relayed through Will's translation.

After spending nearly an hour with Mr. Harper, they were relieved to get back outside and into the fresh air. But their time with Mr. Harper had proved valuable. They had learned that Red Buffalo and his people would be allotted 640 acres in a grassy valley about three miles outside of town. Mr. Harper gave Red Buffalo a handwritten note with his signature. This note gave them the legal claim to the land. The land was surrounded by hills and cut in two by the Illinois River so they would have a consistent source of fresh water. This would be their new home.

Over the rest of the long hot summer, Will helped Red Buffalo and his people get established. They walked the land and carefully surveyed it, planning out where their permanent family lodges would be built, leaving room in the middle for the large council lodge where the elders would meet. They figured out where they would plant their crops and where they would pasture their livestock. And whenever they needed things from town, Will would go with them to help translate. Will even began to teach the children how to speak English so they could help their parents understand the strange new language.

Will's days were full. He'd meet first thing in the morning with the elders in the council lodge for planning and organizing. Then he'd spend the day helping to clear land for planting or pasturing. After a full day of hard work, he'd gather the children for their tutoring. He'd never felt so fulfilled in his life. In fact, he was so busy that he barely had time to realize that he was living the life he'd always dreamed he'd be living.

But there were days when loneliness surprised him. He missed his family. He missed the farm and ol' Blue. He even missed feeding the hogs. Sometimes, whether he was working or sleeping, the longing washed over him. But his life was different now. He knew he would never go back to the farm and the old ways of doing things.

When the dark cloud of loneliness settled on him, he would take Spirit out for a ride. That's when he felt closest to Son, when he was out on the trail riding Spirit. He could hear Son's voice in the wind, encouraging and cheering him on. After an hour or so on Spirit, the dark clouds would vanish.

It was early fall and the leaves on the trees were just beginning to show their autumn colors. The evening sky was gray and dripping with a light drizzle. Grandpa would call this a "soft Irish" day, Will thought. He saddled up for a ride. He rode Spirit along the main road out of the new village but instead of heading into town, he took a left at the fork and headed up into the hills. The trail wound through the trees on a path covered with the first of the fallen yellow leaves. The trail led them up to a meadow at the top of the hill. The last of the season's wildflowers spread like a colorful carpet across the meadow.

Will and Spirit stopped and took in the view. He could see the village below that represented weeks of hard work and planning. He saw wisps of smoke from the cook fires climbing up into the wet sky. He was reminded about the first time he saw these people on that first ride to the village with Son. It seemed like such a long time ago. There was peace and happiness now and Will felt good inside knowing he was able to help. He raised his eyes and looked out to the horizon. Even though the sky was gray, the sun was peeking out from under the heavy blanket of clouds just one last time before it set behind the hills.

Will took a deep breath and tugged his duster collar up around his neck to ward off the evening's chill. He knew it was time now to move on. There was an itch inside that warned him against getting too comfortable, too settled in to these surroundings. Will knew settling wasn't the life for him. He was a pioneer and he knew there were others out there, over that next hill, who needed him too. His work was far from over.

He reached inside his coat to the inside breast pocket and pulled out a folded sheet of paper. It was wrinkled and worn, soft from being handled so much. It seemed like a long time ago he'd found Son's letter on his desk. Now, he opened it and read Son's words over again. The ink was faded but Will could just make it out in the evening light. "*Remember, there's always an adventure over the next hill.*" Will smiled and refolded the letter and put it safely back in his pocket.

He reached down and ran his fingers through the horse's thick mane, patted his neck and said, "You ready Spirit?" The jet black horse snorted, nodded his head and pawed the ground with his giant hoof. "Yeah, you're ready. You're always ready." Will smiled and watched as the last of the sun's rays dipped below the distant hills. He reined Spirit around to head back to the village. His heart ached when he thought about saying good-bye, but there was something else. His heart also soared to think about what was out there in front of him. He knew that there were other rivers to cross and other hills to climb. He knew there were new adventures waiting for him out there.

It was time to go.

Epilogue

The keys jangled at the sheriff's side as he went back to fetch his prisoners. It was Hanging Day and it was time to prepare the men for the last long walk to the gallows.

Two of his prisoners were lifelong criminals and were quickly found to be guilty. But the other one… he was a strange case indeed. He'd endured the long trial just sitting in his chair, barely uttering a word in his own defense. The jury spent less than an hour in deliberations and had come back with the guilty verdict, sentencing him to hang.

The sheriff thought at the time it was a harsh sentence. But he figured the prisoner knew what he was doing and if he didn't want to hang, he shouldn't have been helping the Indians.

He took one of the giant keys and unlocked the heavy door. All three of his prisoners were scheduled to hang. It would be a long day with endless paper-work and fussy town officials to deal with, each with their own long list of tedious questions. It's funny, the sheriff thought, they all wanted the three prisoners to hang, but now that the day was here they were all try-ing to distance themselves from the grim decision.

He walked the length of the hallway leading back to the jail cells. It was early and the morning sun was only now starting to shed it's light on the shadows. The sheriff cleared his throat, jangled the keys and called out, "Time to rise and shine gents! Your last meal will be here shortly. Time to get up and get ready. You don't want to be late for your own hanging!"

The sheriff walked past the first cell and could see the prisoner rouse himself in the shadows. As he continued down the narrow hallway, he peered in the middle cell but didn't see any movement. He heard the prisoner in the last cell banging around getting ready for his last day.

He took the keys and rattled them loudly in front of the middle cell door. "Get up Son! You're going to be the center of attention today hanging between these two lowlifes!"

There was still no movement in the darkness of the middle cell.

"GET UP SON!" the sheriff yelled, now losing his patience. It was still too dark to see much so he grabbed a lantern off the hook on the wall and lit it. He held it up, casting it's light into the dark cell. Nothing. He gritted his teeth. That's all he needed... a prisoner trying to hide. Now he'd have to drag him out and show him who was boss in this town!

The sheriff set the lantern on the floor and unlocked the door. He picked the lantern back up and entered the cell holding it high hoping to see if his prisoner was crouched in the corner or under his bunk.

But the cell was empty! The only thing left of Son was his nightshirt draped across the cot.

"Where'd he go?" the sheriff bellowed.

"What're you yellin' about sheriff?" asked the first prisoner.

"Son ain't in here! You two better start talking! Where'd he go?"

"We can't see over there and we didn't hear a thing," moaned the second prisoner. "You're saying he ain't in his cell no more?"

"I'm saying he vanished! The cell was locked when I got here. Now you tell me where he went!"

"We don't know nothin' Sheriff. We didn't hear a thing!" said the first prisoner.

He continued to pepper the two prisoners with questions but realized they didn't know anymore than he did. The fact was, Son had simply vanished into thin air. How in the world was he going to explain this to the judge?

He walked back to his office forgetting to fetch breakfast for his two remaining prisoners. He slumped into his chair, his shoulders heavy with the new responsibility of a missing prisoner. There was no getting around it. He would have to organize a posse and go searching for Son. But where could he have gone? There were no clues. Just an empty cell.

How could Son have just escaped into thin air?

Author Biography

Based out of Tulsa, Oklahoma, Michael Staires is happily married with seven children and one grandchild. A pioneer at heart and a born storyteller, it's not surprising that while serving as camp director at Shepherd's Fold Ranch for many years, one of his most popular tales was a western yarn about a young boy who dreams of becoming a kind and heroic cowboy like his uncle. Expertly melding spiritual lessons with thrilling adventures, *A Long Ride Home* is the first book in the Billy Christian series. Michael can be found online at www.mstaires.com.

40912340R00099

Made in the USA
Charleston, SC
19 April 2015